Brilliant Publications

Fun with
Plays

Brilliant Publications

Contents

Introduction

All children, even the most reluctant readers, love reading playscripts. Reao·
playscripts aloud, in groups, is a tremendous way to boost their reading
abilities. One of the reasons for this as that **all** of the children involved in any
script have to read **all** of the script as it's unfolding to make sure that they don't
miss their own turn. They also enjoy rereading and taking the parts of different
characters – whereas if you ask them to reread a piece of narrative or reference
material you are definitely asking them to do something that is viewed as hard
work!

This book of playscripts has been specially written for children aged 7–11 years,
to fit in with the National Literacy Strategy. Its companion book is **Fun with Poems**
and within the two you will find much of the material you need for your Literacy
Hour lessons.

It is not intended that the children should try to produce the scripts as plays,
though, of course, if they have the time and inclination to do so, it will enhance
their reading. Rather they should see the reading itself as a kind of
performance – this will involve them in working out how the lines should be
read and making the best use of expression.

Your pupils should be encouraged to:

■ Read through each play silently, alone.

■ Check for any words they may have difficulty with.

■ Read the play aloud in a group as a 'first draft' reading.

■ Write comments in the margins to help them with the second reading.

■ Reread the play, using the right kind of voice for each character.

■ Change roles and read the part of a different character.

■ Discuss the scripts and try to work out their themes (that is, the message
behind them).

You may need to explain the following concepts:

■ Dialogue – the words that each character says. These words can also
be called the character's 'speeches'.

- Props – short for 'properties'. Properties are anything that need to be on stage, ranging from chairs, goalposts, walls, scarecrows, etc. to smaller things like footballs, bags of crisps, torches, etc. which can be carried on stage (these are called 'hand props').
- Scenes – a playscript can be divided into several scenes – each scene takes place either in a different location or at a different time, or both.
- Scripts – a script is the pages of text.
- Set – the setting of the play – for example is it a football pitch, a farm, a spaceship – or where?
- Stage directions – these are the bits of text which are not dialogue but which tell the actors things about the scene or about expression – for instance, they might say that the character enters (comes on stage or set) or exits (leaves the stage or set) or speaks loudly, quietly, angrily, etc.
- Voices off – one or more voices which are not part of the play or script giving the audience information.
- Cue – the words directly before the words you are going to read aloud.

Links with the NLS

Whilst **playscripts** are actually prescribed reading only within Year 3 Term 1, Year 4 Term I and Year 5 Term I, it is our view that all of the plays can be called **fiction** as well as playscripts. These scripts have been written particularly to provide fiction texts for group reading within the ranges of texts that are suggested reading for each term. Please note that no one associated with this book would suggest that any playscript should be used only during a certain term or at a certain time. We show below the terms into which they fit most easily within the guidelines of the NLS – but that is not because we think they should be used ONLY at those times: it is meant merely as helpful input for the teacher.

Thus:

Year 3, Term 1 – Stories with familiar settings;
Read:
Jennifer Jenks and her Excellent Day Out
Feet First
Saving Blister
Back Chat
Dog in the Car.

Year 3, Term 2 – Myths, legends, fables, parables; traditional stories, stories with related themes.
Read:
Kadu's Magic Gourd
Aladdin and the Magic Lamp
Loki the Mischief Maker.

Year 3, Term 3 – Adventure and mystery stories; stories by the same author.
Read:
Saving Blister
Playing Away
The Ghost of Sir Hubert.
All scripts – there are two plays by each of five authors.

Year 4, Term 1 – playscripts.
Read:
All scripts.

Year 4, Term 2 – stories about imagined worlds: fantasy adventures.
Read:
Saving Blister
Playing Away
The Ghost of Sir Hubert.

Year 4, Term 3 – stories that raise issues; stories from other cultures.
Read:
Kadu's Magic Gourd
Saving Blister
Playing Away
Aladdin and the Magic Lamp
Loki the Mischief Maker.

Year 5, Term 1 – playscripts.
Read:
All scripts.

Year 5, Term 2 – traditional stories, myths, legends, fables from a range of cultures.
Read:
Kadu's Magic Gourd
Aladdin and the Magic Lamp
Loki the Mischief Maker.

Year 5, Term 3 – stories from a variety of cultures and traditions.
Read:
All scripts.

Year 6, Term 1– classic fiction and drama by long-established authors.
Read:
The Ghost of Sir Hubert as an introduction to **A Midsummer Night's Dream** by William Shakespeare.

Year 6, Term 2 – stories from more than one genre to compare.
Read:
All scripts.

Year 6, Term 3 – work by the same author.
Read:
All scripts – there are two plays by each of five authors.

Each play has an introduction with ideas for reading and performing the script. These introductions are written to be helpful and indicative of how the scripts should be read and to provide a different kind of reading for the pupils.

At the back of the book are some photocopiable worksheets which can be used to provide text-related work.

Jennifer Jenks
and her Excellent Day Out

by Paul Copley

This play is called a performance poem because it has quite a strict rhyming pattern and form in some places, and because it is so obviously meant to be read aloud. If you read it well (and fast) enough, it will rollick along and be great fun.

You can make a big issue out of the onomatopoeia (words which make the sound they say) for example, CLONK! BANG! RUMBLE! The more effort you put into them, the better your performance will be. The play also has lots of alliteration (words beginning with the same sounds) so make the most of that when you are reading aloud.

Would you be able to perform this play on stage? You could easily work out a set, and it would be quite simple to use chairs, for instance, as the car and to act Pa driving with the car going along. You could make cardboard buckets, pigs, hens, etc. for the farm and even a big cardboard farmhouse. In fact, cardboard cut-outs would be in keeping with the spirit of the play and make it great fun.

Think about the stage directions – do they need to be read aloud or can the script readers just read them in their heads? If they do need to be read aloud, how are you going to incorporate this?

Things to talk about:
- What kind of family do you think the Jenks family is?
- What makes you form your opinions about them?
- What difference do the rhymes and rhythms make to the play compared to a play written in ordinary narrative text?
- What do you like best about the script? Why?

This page may be photocopied for use by the purchasing institution only.

Brilliant Publications – Fun with Plays
Jennifer Jenks and her Excellent Day Out by Paul Copley

7

Jennifer Jenks
and her Excellent Day Out

by Paul Copley

Cast:

Jen
Jack
Ma
Pa
Granpa
Granma

Brilliant Publications – Fun with Plays
Jennifer Jenks and her Excellent Day Out by Paul Copley

Scene 1	**In the Jenks' kitchen**

(Enter Jen

Jen: Hello.
I'm Jennifer.
Jennifer Jenks. It's Saturday, shout hurray!

Pa's mended the car,
With some help from Ma,
And we're all going out for the day!

Now, where's my brother!
(calling) JACK! JACK JENKS! ARE YOU READY YET?

(Enter Jack)

Jack: There's no need to shout! I'm right here behind you.

Jen: Ooh! So you are!

But you're late. You're late.
You're always late.
That's why I gave you a shout!

We must be away
Before mid-day
And it's time we were starting out!

Jack: Did you find out where we are going?

Jen: Well... Ma won't say
And Pa won't say
They want it to be a surprise

Jack: A mystery jaunt
To a seaside haunt!
That's my guess, do you think likewise?

Jen: No. **(whispers)** Because I heard Ma and Pa talking
about going to see Granma.

Jack: We're going to see Granma?

Jen:	Sssh! Yes, I think so.
Jack:	Great! So we will see Granpa too.
Jen:	And we will see their new house.
Jack:	It's not a house, it's a farm!
Jen:	It's a farmhouse.
Jack:	Pa said they've gone to live on a farm! Bramble Farm!
Jen:	Alright, they live ON a farm, but IN a farmhouse!

**(Enter Ma, very quietly.
Jen and Jack do not see her)**

Jack: They live on a farm
But not in a barn
And their house is called the farmhouse!

(He links arms with Jen)

Arm in arm
To Bramble Farm
We're going to Bramble Farmhouse!

(She takes away her arm)

Jen:	Shush Jack! Remember, it's a surprise. So be surprised when they tell us.
Jack:	I'll remember.
Jen:	Now, it's getting late. Where's Ma?

Jack: She's late. She's late.
She's always late.
We'll have to give her a shout!

Jen: We must be away
Before mid-day
And it's time we were starting out!

Jack:	Ready?
Jen:	Steady?
Jen/Jack:	**(shouting)** MA! MA JENKS! ARE YOU READY YET?
Ma:	There's no need to shout. I'm right here behind you.
Jen/Jack:	Ooh! So you are!
Ma:	Are you both ready to go?
Jen/Jack:	YES WE ARE!
Ma:	Then you had better link arms!
Jen:	Why?
Jack:	What do you mean Ma?
Ma:	Arm in arm? To Bramble Farm?
Jack:	Oh no, you heard my rhyme!
Ma:	Of course, because You see, I was Behind you all the time!
Jack:	Sorry Ma. But it's still a smashing surprise!
Jen:	It'll be an excellent day out!
Ma:	Come on then, let's go! Wait a minute! Where's Pa?
Jack:	He WILL be late.
Ma:	He's BOUND to be late.
Jen/Jack/Ma:	He's ALWAYS late!
	(Enter Pa)
Pa:	Hello everybody! Are you waiting for me?

This page may be photocopied for use
by the purchasing institution only.

Brilliant Publications – Fun with Plays
Jennifer Jenks and her Excellent Day Out by Paul Copley

11

Jen/Jack/Ma:	You're late. You're late. You're always late. We're ALWAYS waiting for you!
Jack:	Where were you Pa?
Pa:	I was in the car, And I was waiting for you!
Ma:	We should all stop grumbling!
Pa:	Jack, what are you mumbling?
Jack:	I'll race you all out to the car!
Ma:	Well, I'm on my feet.
Jen:	Jack will get the front seat!
Pa:	You can sit in the back like a star!

(They all leave)

Scene 2	**In the car**

(Ma and Jack sit in the front, Ma driving, while Pa and Jen sit in the back seats)

Ma:	Right you lot! I'm driving.
Pa:	Off we go then, to Granma and Granpa's new house.
Jack:	Their new farmhouse!
Pa:	That's right Jack. I saw it last week when I helped them move in. They've always wanted to live on a farm.
Ma:	And now they've got one of their very own. Ready everybody?
Jen/Jack/Pa:	YES WE ARE!
Ma:	Start the engine
Pa:	Hear it hum!
Jack:	Look out Granma

Jennifer Jenks and her Excellent Day Out by Paul Copley

Jen:	Here we come!
Ma:	Beep Beep!
Jack:	Rumble Rumble!
Pa:	Clonk Clonk!
Jen:	Bang!
Ma:	Beep Beep!
Jack:	Rumble Rumble!
Pa:	Clonk Clonk!
Jen:	Bang!
Jen/Jack:	BEEP BEEP, RUMBLE RUMBLE, CLONK CLONK, BANG!
Jen/Jack/Ma/Pa:	BEEP BEEP, RUMBLE RUMBLE, CLONK CLONK, BANG!

Scene 3	**On the farm**

(Granpa is waiting to greet everybody)

(Enter Jen, Jack, Ma and Pa)

Jack:	Hello Granpa!
Granpa:	Welcome to Bramble Farm everybody!
Jen:	Thank you Granpa!
Granpa:	How was the car journey?
Jack:	Well, the engine grumbled,
Jen:	And the wheels rumbled,
Ma:	But the car got us here...
Pa:	... and out we all tumbled!

This page may be photocopied for use
by the purchasing institution only.

Brilliant Publications – Fun with Plays
Jennifer Jenks and her Excellent Day Out by Paul Copley

13

Jen:	Where's Granma Jenks?
Granpa:	She's feeding the hens. You see Jen, Granma and I have never run a farm before.

We enjoy it, it's true
But there's so much to do
That it takes up a lot of our time

	Gran's running late!
Ma:	That's OK, we can wait.
Pa:	Look out Ma, you've trod in some slime!
Ma:	Ooops!!
Jen:	You say Granma's feeding the hens?
Granpa:	That's right. Would you like to see?
Jen/Jack:	YES PLEASE!
Granpa:	Follow me then!

(They all follow him)

We go through the cowshed...

Jack:	MOOO-OOO!
Pa:	Round the duckpond...
Jack:	QUACK! QUACK!
Ma:	And into the hen-run...
Jen:	COCK-A-DOODLE-DOO!
Jack:	MOOO-OOO! QUACK QUACK!
Jen:	COCK-A-DOODLE-DOO!
Jack:	MOOO-OOO! QUACK QUACK!

Brilliant Publications – Fun with Plays
Jennifer Jenks and her Excellent Day Out by Paul Copley

Jen:	COCK-A-DOODLE-DOO !
Jen/Jack:	MOOO-OOO! QUACK QUACK!! COCK-A-DOODLE-DOO! MOOO-OOO! QUACK QUACK!! COCK-A-DOODLE-DOO!
	(Enter Granma carrying a bucket)
Granpa:	And here's Granma Jenks...
Jen/Jack:	Hi Granma!
Granma:	Hello everybody!
Ma/Pa:	Hi Granma!
Granma:	Just look at me! Surrounded by my flock of hens – They were scratching and fratching And flapping about I just rattled the bucket and gave them a shout!
Jen:	It's lovely here Granma. We didn't know you had all these cows and ducks and hens and things!
Jack:	Yeh, it's smashing Gran!
Granma:	Thanks you two, I'm glad you like our farm. Well, shall we go inside the house?
Jack:	Er... go inside the house?
Jen:	Gran don't be a tease Let's stay outside please You've got animals galore we can see!
Granpa:	There's our pony called Twiglet. My cows, and Gran's piglet. Why, even the cat's got a flea!
Ma:	We'd like to look round too, wouldn't we Pa?
Pa:	We would, and we'd like to help, wouldn't we Jack?

Jack: Yes please, we can help with all sorts of jobs!

Jen: Please can we help, Granma?

Granma: Of course you can!

Granpa: You can all lend a hand!

Pa: Oops! Watch your step Ma!
You've trod in the mud
If you sink down much more you'll take root!

Ma: Ooh I'm stuck, what a mess
All over my dress
Oh no! I've just lost my boot!

Pa: Quick Jack!

Jack: Come on Jen!

Jen: Grab hold Granpa!

Pa: And we'll pull Ma out of the mud!

Brilliant Publications – Fun with Plays
Jennifer Jenks and her Excellent Day Out by Paul Copley

(They form a chain taking hold of each other round the waist. Granma stands back to watch)

Jen: Ready!

Jack: Steady!

Jen/Jack/Pa/Granpa: HEAVE!

(Ma does not move very much)

Granma: And again!

Jen: Ready!

Jack: Steady!

Jen/Jack/Pa/Granpa: HEAVE!

(This time they pull Ma out of the mud)

Ma: Ooh! Dry land! Thanks everybody!

**Jen/Jack/Pa/Ma
Granpa/Granma:** HURRAY!

Ma: Right, who's going to volunteer to fetch my boot out of the mud?

Jen: We don't have to Ma. Look, Granpa's dog is pulling it out for you.

Granpa:	Well done Rover, here boy! Good lad!
Jen:	Yes, well done Rover Oh don't roll over! I don't want that mud on me!
Granma:	Ha-ha! When it's dry You must see the pigsty, First – let's have a nice cup of tea!
Jen:	Three cheers for Granma and Granpa and Beautiful Bramble Farm! Hip, hip...
Jen/Jack/Pa/Ma:	HURRAY!
Jack:	Hip, hip...
Jen/Jack/Pa/Ma:	HURRAY!
Jen/Jack:	HIP, HIP...
Jen/Jack/Pa/Ma:	HURRAY!

(They all laugh and leave for a cup of tea)

Scene 4	**Back in the car**

(This time Pa and Jen sit in the front, Pa driving, while Ma and Jack sit in the back seats)

Ma:	Pa's turn to drive!
Jen:	My turn in the front!
Pa:	Wave goodbye to Granma and Granpa!
Jen/Jack/Ma:	GOODBYE – EEEEE!
Granpa/Granma:	GOODBYE – EEEEE! Come again soon!
Jen/Jack:	We will. Thank you!

Pa:	Ready for the trip back home everybody?
Jen/Jack:	YES WE ARE!
Ma:	Start the engine
Pa:	Hear it hum
Jen:	Look out our house
Jack:	Here we come!
Ma:	Beep Beep!
Jack:	Rumble Rumble!
Pa:	Clonk Clonk!
Jen:	Bang!
Ma:	Beep Beep!
Jack:	Rumble Rumble!
Pa:	Clonk Clonk!
Jen:	Bang!
Jen/Jack:	BEEP BEEP, RUMBLE RUMBLE, CLONK CLONK, BANG!
Jen/Jack/Ma/Pa:	BEEP BEEP, RUMBLE RUMBLE, CLONK CLONK, BANG!
Ma:	Ooh, I had such a laugh Collecting the eggs.
Jack:	I saw a scarecrow with flapping legs!
Pa:	You LOOK like a scarecrow In Granpa's old jeans!
Jack:	Well I couldn't wear mine after where they had been!
Ma:	Still, you did feed the pigs. Of that we have proof!
Jen:	You sat down in the pigsty, you great big goof!

Brilliant Publications – Fun with Plays
Jennifer Jenks and her Excellent Day Out by Paul Copley

19

Jack:	I tripped over the cat! And just went down, SPLAT!
Pa:	There was a horrible stink, I can tell you that!

(They all laugh)

Ma:	But we all had a lovely time in the end.
Pa:	I milked a cow!
Jack:	MOOOOO!
Jen:	I fed the ducks!
Pa:	QUACK! QUACK!
Ma:	Jack fed the pigs!
Jen:	GRUNT! GRUNT!
Jack:	And... I fell over in the pigsty!
Ma:	SPLOSH!

(They all laugh again)

Jen:	What an excellent day out! When can we go back to Bramble Farm Pa?
Pa:	Granpa said you can visit whenever you like!
Ma:	Granma said you could both stay with them in the summer holidays!
Jack:	Hurray!
Jen:	Bramble Farm is my favourite place in the whole world! We can milk the cows!
Jack:	MOOOOO!
Jen:	And feed the ducks!

Brilliant Publications – Fun with Plays
Jennifer Jenks and her Excellent Day Out by Paul Copley

Pa:	QUACK! QUACK!
Jen:	And feed the pigs!
Ma:	GRUNT! GRUNT!
Jen:	And fall over in the pigsty!
Jack:	SPLOSH!
Pa:	We're nearly there We're nearly home
Ma:	I'm ready for my tea!
Jen:	To pass the time Let's chant a rhyme That's as silly as silly can be! Ready!
Jack:	Steady!
Pa:	MOOOOO!
Jen:	QUACK! QUACK!
Jack:	GRUNT! GRUNT!
Ma:	SPLOSH!
Jen/Jack:	MOOOOO! QUACK! QUACK! GRUNT! GRUNT! SPLOSH!
Ma/Pa:	MOOOOO! QUACK! QUACK! GRUNT! GRUNT! SPLOSH!
Jen/Jack/Ma/Pa:	MOOOOO! QUACK! QUACK! GRUNT! GRUNT! SPLOSH!

(They all laugh and shout HURRAY!)

This page may be photocopied for use
by the purchasing institution only.

Brilliant Publications – Fun with Plays
Jennifer Jenks and her Excellent Day Out by Paul Copley

21

Feet First

by Trevor Harvey

This script is a very quick one that is really just a conversation between six children. It's the kind of conversation any of group of you might have at any time.

It assumes that you understand the difference between several roles on the football pitch, and several roles off the football pitch.

When you read this playscript aloud you need to make sure there are no pauses or awkward silences, except where there are supposed to be.

It would be a very easy play to perform. What would you need for a set? What props would you need? After reading, talk about the play together and decide how easily you could perform it.

Things to talk about:

- The six children are a group of friends. Why do you think they are friends?
- Do you think there is a 'leader'?
- Who do you think the leader is?
- Why?
- What points does the play make about earning lots of money?

Feet First

by Trevor Harvey

Cast : **Warren**
Susie
Malik
Rema
Andrew
Janet

A group of children are sitting on a wall in a park. From time to time, two of them stand up and dribble a football to one another.

Warren:	**(He is eating from a packet of crisps)** When I grow up, I'm going to be a goalkeeper...
Janet:	A goalkeeper!
Andrew:	You don't even get picked for the school team! You'll never be ANY kind of footballer. You've got two left feet, that's why!
Warren:	No I haven't! Look! **(He takes off his right shoe and sock)**
Rema:	Pooh! What's that smell of cheese?
Andrew:	Quick! Put your sock back on! **(Warren replaces his sock and shoe)**
Malik:	Anyway, goalkeepers need a 'safe' pair of hands.
Warren:	That's all right. I know where mine are. **(He waves them)** See?
Susie:	**(She is nibbling at a biscuit and has a packet in her hand)** Sorry, Warren. You're no good as a goalie. You're no good as a defender. You're no good as a striker. Andrew's right – you WON'T be a footballer when you leave school.
Rema:	You could always be a referee.
Andrew:	He couldn't. He wears glasses already.
Malik:	You could become an agent... for footballers. There was a programme on TV about a man who was an agent.
Rema:	What did he do?
Malik:	He rode around in a big posh car.

 Brilliant Publications – Fun with Plays
Feet First by Trevor Harvey

Susie: I saw that programme! He ate hamburgers whenever he wanted!

Warren: Great! That's the life for me.

Janet: Your Mum won't let you drive a car.

Warren: I could ride on my bike.

Janet: Anyway, you don't like hamburgers.

Warren: Who cares? I could eat cheeseburgers.

Andrew: Ugh! Then your feet would smell even WORSE!

Susie: I think I'LL become a footballers' agent.

Malik: GIRLS can't be agents!

Susie: Why not? Girls are BETTER at playing football than some BOYS are!

Andrew: Yeah?

Susie: Yeah! So I'm sure I'll be a better agent, as well!

Warren: Prove it!

Susie: What?

Malik: Prove you're better than Warren.

Warren: Dare you!

Susie: All right! How?

Malik: Both of you could be footballers' agents – right now!

Rema: They're not old enough.

Malik: WE play football, don't we? They can be agents for us.

Andrew: But, when we play, it's ONLY three aside!

This page may be photocopied for use by the purchasing institution only.

Brilliant Publications – Fun with Plays
Feet First by Trevor Harvey

25

Malik: So?

Rema: Do it, Susie!

Janet: Go for it, Warren!

Malik: Is it a deal?

Susie: Done!

Warren: Right – who wants ME as their agent? **(Silence)** Don't all rush, will you?

Susie: I expect they want ME instead. **(Silence)**

Rema: Will it cost us anything?

Susie: No. We're only pretending.

Malik: And agents work out good deals with football team managers, so the players get paid lots of money.

Andrew: Cor – THAT sounds good!

Malik: Listen – get into two teams. Warren will be the Agent for the players in one team – and Susie will be the agent for the players in the other. All right?

(They make two lines. Malik and Andrew stand near Warren, Rema and Janet stand near Susie)

Andrew: Good idea.

Janet: I'm joining Susie's team.

Rema: Stop pushing!

Malik: There's no need to fight!
(They stand still)

Susie: Well... I've got TWO people in my team...

Warren:	And I've got TWO in mine.
Janet:	I'm a goalie.
Andrew:	So am I.
Malik:	I want to be a defender.
Rema:	So do I.
Susie:	Two goalies and two defenders! It won't be much of a game, will it?
Warren:	So, what happens now?
Malik:	YOU should know. You're our agents!
Warren:	But I don't know what agents do.
Malik:	I told you, they look after their players. Make sure they have what they want.
Andrew:	Right! Give me one of your crisps, Warren. I'm hungry. My stomach's making noises.
Janet:	And I'll have one of your biscuits, please, Susie.
Warren:	Tough! **(Warren hides his crisps)**
Susie:	That's what you YOU think! **(Susie hides her biscuits) (pause)**
Rema:	Who's my team manager?
Andrew:	Yeah – who's mine?
Malik:	Warren is.
Andrew:	What... ?
Malik:	Warren's YOUR Team Manager, Andrew – AND he's also mine. Susie will have to be the team manager for Rema and Janet.

Susie:	But I thought I was supposed to be an AGENT?
Warren:	So did I!
Malik:	We haven't enough people to go around. You'll have to be our team managers as well as our agents.
Janet:	Right! I want a pay rise, Susie!
Susie:	What... ?
Janet:	You're my team manager – I want a pay rise!
Rema:	So do I.
Andrew:	And what about MY pay, Warren? How much will I get?
Warren:	We only have a 'knockabout' in the park. Who's going to pay anyone for doing THAT!
Malik:	You could charge people to watch.
Susie:	No one in their right mind would watch us play!
Warren:	Anyway, we don't even have proper goalposts. We roll up a couple of coats.
Malik:	The people whose coats we use will want paying as well.
Warren:	Not likely! I'm not paying ANYONE!
Susie:	I'm not, either!
Andrew:	In that case – I'm going on strike! **(He sits down, arms folded)**
Rema:	Me, too! **(She sits)**
Janet:	Good idea! **(She sits)**
Malik:	Sorry, Warren! **(He sits)**

Susie:	What's happening?
Janet:	We won't kick another ball until you give us what we want.
Susie:	How are we meant to do THAT?
Malik:	You're our agents, so think of something. Arrange a meeting with our team managers.
Warren:	We ARE the team managers!
Susie:	That means we'll have to talk to OURSELVES!
Malik:	That's right.
Andrew:	Well? What's the answer?
Warren:	The same as it was five minutes ago!
Rema:	Susie... ?
Susie:	I agree with Warren.
Andrew:	Sorry, Warren – but I think you're RUBBISH!
Janet:	You don't make a good team manager, Susie –
Rema:	I don't like you as my agent, either!
Malik:	HOPELESS! Now you've made EVERYBODY unhappy.
Warren:	We can't help it. So, what happens now? Is it a stalemate?
Malik:	No it isn't. Find some different players.
Susie:	But there aren't any!
Malik:	There are! How about the transfer market? I don't want WARREN as my manager, so I could become one of YOUR players, Susie.
Susie:	O.K.!

This page may be photocopied for use by the purchasing institution only.

Brilliant Publications – Fun with Plays
Feet First by Trevor Harvey

29

Malik:	You need to make it worth my while. What will you give me if I change to your side?
Susie:	Er... You can have one of my biscuits, if you like.
Malik:	Thanks! **(She holds out the packet; he takes one)**
Warren:	Hey – that's not fair!
Andrew:	I'll swop for a biscuit, as well!
Susie:	All right. **(She holds out the packet; Andrew takes one; he and Malik join Susie)**
Janet:	What about us?
Rema:	Yes. Don't we get one?
Susie:	Sorry – you're both on strike.
Janet:	In that case, I want to join WARREN'S side!

Rema:	So do I! **(They change places to join Warren)**
Warren:	Good!
Janet:	It'll cost you a crisp. **(Warren reluctantly holds out crisps to Janet)**
Rema:	Me, too! **(Warren holds out crisps to Rema)**
Susie:	NOW what happens?
Andrew:	I think you tell us how much money we'll be paid.
Janet:	For playing football.
Warren:	I'm not paying you ANYTHING!
Susie:	Me, neither!
Andrew:	You mean, nothing has changed?
Susie:	No. The only thing that's happened is YOU'VE changed sides!
Malik:	I think I liked it better when I was with Warren.
Andrew:	Me, too!
Janet:	I liked Susie.
Rema:	So did I. **(They change places again)**
Warren:	Hang on! What's happening now?
Janet:	We're changing back again.
Susie:	Changing back?
Malik:	Yes. At a price!
Warren:	WHAT price?
Malik:	TWO crisps this time.

This page may be photocopied for use by the purchasing institution only.

Brilliant Publications – Fun with Plays
Feet First by Trevor Harvey

31

Warren:	**(surprised)** TWO crisps...?
Malik:	Done! **(He takes them, then passes two crisps to Andrew)**
Andrew:	Thanks, Warren.
Rema:	**(To Susie)** And TWO biscuits for us, Susie – then YOU can be OUR Agent again.
Janet:	Sounds great to me! **(Janet takes the packet from Susie, helps herself to two biscuits and passes two biscuits to Rema)**
Malik:	**(eating his crisps)** Well, did you enjoy being agents... ?
Susie:	Not much!
Warren:	You haven't said who you liked – Susie or me?
Janet:	I'm not sure yet.
Malik:	I can't make up MY mind, either.
Rema:	At first I liked Warren –
Andrew:	– and then I liked Susie.
Malik:	I think we'll have to come back tomorrow – then we can try again.
Rema:	Good idea! Same time –
Janet:	– same place.
Malik:	Is that all right, Warren...? **(Warren nods)** Susie – ?
Susie:	NO! I'm fed up with being an agent and a manager! Tomorrow, SOMEONE ELSE can show us how to do it PROPERLY.
Malik:	What do you mean?

Susie:	Tomorrow, TWO OTHER PEOPLE should be the agents and managers. Then Warren and I can WATCH – and learn from our mistakes! Tomorrow we can pretend WE'RE members of the football team.
Warren:	Right! **(pleased)** Wicked!
Susie:	How about it, Malik? I think it's YOUR turn to be one of the agents and managers.
Malik:	**(unsure)** Well...
Warren:	And Janet can be the other one! Go on I DARE you!
Malik:	Oh – all right! Janet – ?
Janet:	I suppose so!
Susie:	Good! And one other thing... Malik... Janet... Now YOU'RE the managers and agents, don't forget to bring plenty of FOOD with you, will you...?
Warren:	Ask your mums if you can have cakes and pizza. They'll be better than biscuits and crisps!
Susie/Rema/ Andrew:	YEAH!
Susie:	And then, the day after, when it's Rema and Andrew's turn, perhaps we could have naan bread and egg sandwiches.
Warren:	Or chicken drumsticks!
Susie/Malik/ Janet:	YEAH!
Susie:	It looks like pretending to be a football manager and agent could end up being quite TASTY!
Rema:	See you tomorrow!
All:	Bye... !

This page may be photocopied for use by the purchasing institution only.

Brilliant Publications – Fun with Plays
Feet First by Trevor Harvey

33

Kadu's Magic Gourd

adapted from an African legend by Moira Andrew

This playscript is adapted from an African legend. As a legend it has a certain quality which makes it not quite as 'real' as, for instance, a play about school might be. Read the play carefully and try to decide what it is about the writing that makes the 'unreal' quality. What kind of messages does the legend carry?

You might be able to perform this play very well with very little setting and props. You could do it in a 'surreal' way, using pictures or very limited costumes, just giving each character one prop or piece of costume to show who they are meant to be.

Things to talk about:

- What makes Kadu decide to do what he does? He is determined and has lots of 'motivation' – there is something that he badly wants to achieve. What is it?
- What do you learn from the incidents with the Grass-cutter and the Water-carrier, from Kadu's first meeting with them and then his second meetings?
- What do you like about the story itself?
- What do you like about the play?

Kadu's Magic Gourd

adapted from an African legend by Moira Andrew

Cast:

Narrator
Grandfather
Kadu
Grass-cutter
Water-carrier
Witch of the Deep Waters

Narrator: Once upon a time, when the world was young, a boy called Kadu lived in a village in Africa. Kadu's grandfather was the village chief and a marvellous storyteller. The boys and girls of the village, Kadu among them, loved to listen to his stories. One night, by a flickering fire, Grandfather told them a story about a magic gourd which was filled with enough good food to feed the world.

Grandfather: Whoever owns the magic gourd will never again need to plant seeds, till the soil or cut corn. It is filled to the brim with all kinds of delicious food.

Kadu: Has this wonderful gourd ever been found, Grandfather?

Grandfather: It has never been found, nor ever will. The gourd is guarded by the Witch of the Deep Waters. She is very fierce and very dangerous and will never let it go.

Narrator: Kadu grew to be a young man. He looked after all the people of the village and saw that everybody had enough to eat. Then a terrible drought came to the land. There was no rain for a whole year. The corn withered, the animals died and still the rains did not come. Then Kadu had a wonderful idea. He went to talk with his grandfather, the wisest man in the village.

Kadu: Grandfather, do you know where the Witch of the Deep Waters lives?

Grandfather: It is said that she lives in a lake beyond the hills.

Kadu: If I could find her, I'd ask her for the magic gourd and bring it back. Then we would all have enough food to eat!

Grandfather: The Witch of the Deep Waters will most likely eat you for supper! But if you must go, try this path first. Someone is sure to know where the witch lives. Take great care and help everybody you meet as you go along. Good luck, my boy!

Narrator:	Kadu set off with some food and a flask of water. He met a man cutting grass and stopped to help him.
Kadu:	My name is Kadu. Is there anything I can do to help you?
Grass-cutter:	Thank you, young man. I could do with some help. I'm getting very tired working in all this heat.
Kadu:	What would you like me to do?
Grass-cutter:	Please pick up the grass stalks as I cut them down. Then put them into bundles, like this.
Narrator:	Kadu and the Grass-cutter worked together until the sun was high in the sky. They were very hungry and thirsty, so they had a drink and the Grass-cutter shared his food with Kadu. When they were rested, Kadu asked about the witch.
Kadu:	Please can you tell me where the Witch of the Deep Waters lives?
Grass-cutter:	That is quite a journey, Kadu! The Witch of the Deep Waters lives far beyond the high blue hills. Take this path down to the river until you meet the Water-carrier. She will tell you the way.
Kadu:	Thank you, my friend.
Grass-cutter:	Take great care, Kadu. The Witch of the Deep Waters is very fierce and very dangerous.
Narrator:	So Kadu set off down a steep stony path towards the river. He went for a very long way. At last he heard the waters of the cool blue river splashing and gurgling among the rocks. When he stopped to rest, Kadu heard someone singing in a soft sweet voice. Then he saw a young girl carrying a jar of water on her head.
Kadu:	Good-day. My name is Kadu. Is there anything I can do to help you?

This page may be photocopied for use
by the purchasing institution only.

Brilliant Publications – Fun with Plays
Kadu's Magic Gourd adapted by Moira Andrew

37

Water-carrier:	Yes please, Kadu. Before nightfall I have to carry a hundred jars of water all the way from the river to the market place. I don't think I can do it without help.
Narrator:	Kadu and the Water-carrier trudged up and down the path from the river to the market place in the village.
	At last they counted the jars – one hundred and one! So they sat down to rest and drank some of the clear cool water.
Water-carrier:	How can I thank you, Kadu?
Kadu:	Please can you tell me where the Witch of the Deep Waters lives?
Water-carrier:	You must go across the high blue hills until you come to a deep black lake. The Witch of the Deep Waters lives in a cave deep down in the lake.
Kadu:	Thank you, my friend.
Water-carrier:	Take great care, Kadu. The Witch of the Deep Waters is very fierce and very dangerous.
Narrator:	Kadu waved good-bye to his friend, the Water-carrier, and set off across the high blue hills. Night was falling. Kadu got very tired indeed. Sometimes he had to stop and rest. Then he remembered the hungry people of his village and trudged on, up and up. At last he saw the deep black waters of the lake, shining and glittering in the moonlight. Kadu felt very frightened, but he gathered his courage, stood on the shores of the lake and shouted at the top of his voice.
Kadu:	Witch of the Deep Waters! Witch of the Deep Waters!
Narrator:	There was no reply, so Kadu tried again.
Kadu:	Witch of the Deep Waters! Can you hear me?
Narrator:	Suddenly there was a noise like a mountain waterfall gushing over rocks and, with a huge splash, a

Narrator: (cont.)	terrible creature rose up from the deep black waters. Her face was thick with mud, her hair green with slime.
Witch:	Who dares call my name?
Kadu:	It is I, Kadu. I have travelled many miles to try and rescue my people. I hope you can help me.
Witch:	And what makes you think that? I don't even know you – or your people!
Kadu:	My grandfather tells me you have a magic gourd, full of delicious food.
Witch:	And what if I have? It has nothing to do with you!
Kadu:	There has been a terrible drought in the land. We have no food to eat and my people are dying. Please may we borrow the magic gourd?
Witch:	Borrow the magic gourd! Indeed, you may not! Let me look at you, boy. You will make a tasty snack. I will eat you for supper!
Narrator:	And with one enormous splash, the Witch of the Deep Waters jumped right out of the lake and grabbed poor Kadu between her thumb and forefinger. Then, still holding Kadu tight, she swam down, down to the very bottom of the deep black lake.
Witch:	Take that, boy!
Narrator:	And, like a gnawed chicken bone, the Witch threw Kadu into the back of a deep black cave. Then she prowled around, looking for something to eat.
Witch:	It's hungry, I am. I'll have a bite to eat and keep that tasty-looking boy for afters!
Narrator:	Kadu watched the witch from a dark corner of the cave. He kept very still and quiet. He saw the witch roll a great golden gourd across the floor. She tapped it

This page may be photocopied for use
by the purchasing institution only.

Brilliant Publications – Fun with Plays
Kadu's Magic Gourd adapted by Moira Andrew

39

Narrator:
(cont.)

once, twice, three times and, sure enough, out spilled enough yams and fruit and corn to feed all the people of Kadu's village for one whole week. Kadu could scarcely believe his eyes. The witch grabbed at the food, stuffing it all into her great wide mouth. She slurped and burped and gurgled. Then she rubbed her round fat stomach.

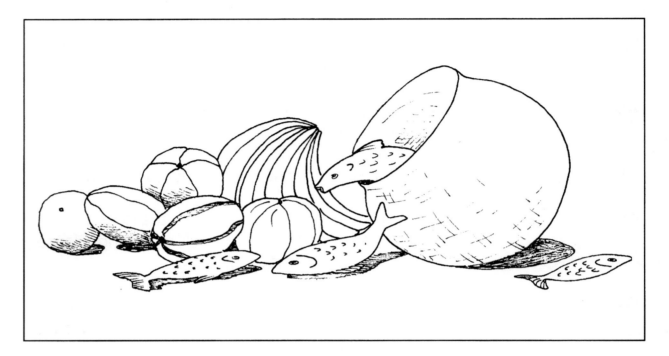

Witch:

That's better! I think I'll doze off for a minute or two before I eat that boy for supper.

Narrator:

The Witch of the Deep Waters fell into a sound sleep, snoring like a great whale. Kadu saw his chance. Carefully, he rolled the great golden gourd to the door of the cave. Then he sat astride it and bobbed like a cork to the top of the deep dark lake.

Kadu:

Come on magic gourd! Let's make for home!

Narrator:

Kadu rolled the gourd down the high blue hills, riding on it. Soon he came to the cool blue river. But the witch had wakened to find both Kadu and the magic gourd gone. She was very angry indeed. She roared like a thunderbolt and her eyes lit up the sky like a flash of lightning.

Witch: Stop thief! Stop thief! Wait till I catch you boy – then you'll be sorry!

Narrator: Kadu saw the Water-carrier waiting by the cool blue river. He felt the witch's hot breath on his neck.

Kadu: Help! Help! The Witch of the Deep Waters is chasing me.

Water-carrier: Don't worry, Kadu. I'll douse her in water from the river.

Narrator: And she did. The river became a torrent, gushing and roaring. The witch gasped and spluttered, but she shook the water from her eyes and kept on going until she almost caught up with Kadu and the gourd. Then Kadu saw the Grass-cutter waiting by the path.

Kadu: Help! Help! The Witch of the Deep Waters is chasing me.

Grass-cutter: Don't worry, Kadu. I'll soon put a stop to her.

Narrator:	The Grass-cutter swirled up great tornadoes of cut grass. The pollen got up the witch's nose and made her sneeze. She sneezed and sneezed and sneezed until she could no longer see where she was going.
Witch:	Atishoo! Atishoo! Atishoo!
Kadu:	Keep going, Gourd! We are almost home!
Narrator:	Kadu rode the great golden gourd along the path and into the village. Grandfather and all the people came out to welcome them.
Grandfather:	Wonderful, my boy! You have been very brave. We are very proud of you and glad to see you home.
Narrator:	Kadu rolled the great golden gourd to a clearing outside Grandfather's hut. He tapped it once, twice, three times, just as the witch had done. The gourd split open and out spilled fish and fruit, corn and spices and all kinds of delicious food. The villagers could hardly believe their eyes.
Kadu:	Come along everyone, come and eat! Eat as much food as you like! As it says in Grandfather's story, never again will you have to plant seeds, till the soil or cut corn – and no-one need ever starve!

Saving Blister

by Stan Barrett

This play has an element of the unexplained, or 'magic', about it. To begin with you might find it very helpful to have an extra voice to read all the stage directions, which are printed in bold type placed in brackets.

Read the play through very carefully then talk about it together to discover what's happening in it and what it all means. At its heart is the issue of bullying. Blister, the bully, gets taught a lesson.

Think about how you could perform this play: you would need several props and the playwright gives you some instructions on how to make the scenes at Wembley, in the balloon and with the bulldozer work.

Things to talk about:
- Do you think the idea of the magic card works?
- Could you retell the rules of the game using the black and white squares or even make up more rules of your own?
- Do you think Blister would learn his lesson from this?
- What do you think Adam felt like to suddenly have some magic power?
- Does the play end in a satisfactory way – what makes it work?

This page may be photocopied for use
by the purchasing institution only.

Brilliant Publications – Fun with Plays
Saving Blister by Stan Barrett

43

Saving Blister

by Stan Barrett

Cast: Narrator
Tracey
Chris
Blister
Adam

Narrator:	Tracey and Chris are standing at the end of Old Wall Street. Each carries a small present and a birthday card.
Blister:	**(from off stage, right)** Hey! You two! Is this where we've got to meet him?
	(They turn and look right)
Tracey and Chris:	**(together)** Blister!
Tracey:	What are you doing here?
	(Enter Blister)
Narrator:	His real name is Barry Lister. He is a bully. He likes his nickname because it makes him sound tough.
Blister:	Where's Adam's birthday party?
Tracey:	But you're not invited.
Blister:	Yes, I am. Told him I'd beat him up if he didn't invite me. Here! What's this? **(he snatches the card from Chris's hand)**
Tracey:	Just you give that back, Blister! That's Adam's birthday card!
Chris:	And it's special. It's magic. The man in the shop said so.
	(Enter Adam. The others do not see him)
Blister:	What shop?
Tracey:	The antique shop.
Blister:	**(scornfully)** That old guy in the junk shop? What a load of rubbish!
Adam:	Hello. **(His voice is rather high and he sounds nervous)** I'm glad you could come.

This page may be photocopied for use by the purchasing institution only.

Brilliant Publications – Fun with Plays
Saving Blister by Stan Barrett

45

Blister:	Here. Have a birthday card.
Tracey:	**(angrily)** That card is from Chris!
Blister:	You'll get mine some other time.
Tracey:	**(quietly)** If you're lucky.
Chris:	Here's my present. Happy birthday, Adam.
Tracey:	And here's my card and a present. Happy birthday.
Adam:	Thanks, everybody.
	(Adam moves to stand with his back to the wall and puts a present under each arm)
Narrator:	Adam opens Chris's card and stares at it. Then he stands up straight and looks more confident.
Blister:	Where's the party?
Adam:	Through this door behind me.
Tracey and Chris:	**(together)** What door?
Adam:	This door.
	(Adam steps away from the wall and stands apart from the rest)
Narrator:	They stare at the old, wooden door in the wall.
Blister:	I've never seen that before.
Adam:	It's heavy. Open it, Blister.
Narrator:	Blister throws himself against the door. Nothing happens. He tries pushing.
	(Chris and Tracey start to giggle)

Blister:	Don't just stand there! Help!
	(All three push against the door)
Narrator:	They don't see Adam put the card on the floor. Then he slips away. **(Pause.)** Suddenly, the door flies open.

(TO THE CAST: From now on impossible things happen. If you want to act this out, you pretend that the impossible things are out there just behind the audience. You make the audience believe you can see these things. Pick spots on the back wall so that your eyes seem to be looking in the right direction when things are described)

	(The three actors go into a short freeze. Then they turn to face the audience and spill on to the floor on hands and knees. It looks as if they have passed through the door and into another world)
Narrator:	They cannot believe their eyes.
Tracey:	**(as she stands)** Where are we?
Chris:	**(he doesn't get up)** I don't know, but it's... it's...
Tracey:	It's beautiful.
Blister:	**(as he stands)** I don't like it. There's nothing behind that wall but old trees and stinging nettles.
Narrator:	Chris doesn't move, but the other two go to explore. There are big black and white tiles under their feet.
Tracey:	It's like walking on a giant chessboard.
Chris:	**(as he stands)** I know where we are.
Blister:	All right. Where are we?
Chris:	This view – it's the one on the pop-up card I gave to Adam.
Tracey:	So where are we?
Chris:	We're inside the birthday card.

This page may be photocopied for use by the purchasing institution only.

Brilliant Publications – Fun with Plays
Saving Blister by Stan Barrett

47

Blister:	INSIDE A BIRTHDAY CARD? Have you gone mad?
	(Chris moves down to the centre of the stage and
looks out)	
Narrator:	Tracey and Blister stand next to Chris and stare.
Chris:	**(points out left)** See that hill covered in trees? That's the same.
Tracey:	And those ponies in the field at the bottom of the hill. Were they there?
Chris:	Yes. **(points right)** And that cottage down there.
Tracey:	Look! Look! That yellow balloon. Can you see it?
Blister:	That's a hot air balloon. I bet that's not on your card.
Chris:	Yes, it is.
Tracey:	**(excited)** It's getting nearer!

Chris:	Look at the ponies. They're galloping round and playing a game.
Blister:	**(pointing)** What about that little bulldozer outside the cottage?
Chris:	That's there.
Tracey:	Hey! What happened to Adam? **(looks round)** He's not here.
Blister:	Yes! Where is Adam? Wait till I get my hands on him! He'll tell us where we are.
	(Adam's voice sounds stronger and deeper. It comes from a distance. He speaks slowly and very clearly)
Adam:	I am here, Blister. I can see you, but you cannot see me. This is my party, so we shall play a game.
Narrator:	The three look in every direction, but there is no sign of Adam.
Blister:	I'm not playing any game. Come out here where I can see you!
Adam:	I think you will like this game, Blister.
	(A big coloured ball rolls on to the stage)
Adam:	Tracey, pick up the ball.
Narrator:	As Tracey picks it up, Adam tells her to throw the ball up high and shout somebody's name.
Adam:	If she shouts your name, you must catch the ball.
Tracey:	**(as she throws the ball)** Chris!
Adam:	**(as Chris catches it)** Well caught, Chris. Now you do the same.
Chris:	Tracey!

(Chris and Tracey throw the ball to each other. After a while...)

Blister: This is boring.

Narrator: As they play, Adam tells them that when he shouts 'Stop!' whoever is holding the ball gets a wish.

Adam: But only if you are standing on a white square.

Chris: What happens if you're on a black square?

Adam: Nothing. We start again.

(The game continues. Nobody calls Blister's name)

Adam: Stop!

Tracey: It's me! And I'm on a white square!

Adam: Look around, Tracey. What is your wish?

Tracey: You see that balloon just landing in the ponies' field? I'd just love to go up in the balloon.

Adam: Easy.

Narrator: Adam tells Tracey to run to the field and the balloon will take off as soon as she is aboard.

(Tracey races off left. Adam restarts the game)

Adam: Go!

Blister: Hang on. Let's see what happens to Tracey.

Narrator: The boys' eyes are wide as they watch Tracey race across to the fields.

Chris: Look! **(points)** She's there. She's getting in.

(Their eyes follow the balloon as it rises)

Chris:	She's waving! **(Chris waves back)**
Adam:	Go!
Blister:	**(he throws the ball so that it is difficult for Chris to catch it)** Get hold of that one!
	(The game continues until...)
Adam:	Stop!
Chris:	I've got it! **(he looks down)** And I'm on a white square! **(pause)** Adam, I don't think you'll be able to do this, but I'd like... I'd like to score the winning goal at a World Cup Final.
Adam:	Easy.
Narrator:	Adam tells Chris there is a flat field just beyond the cottage. When Chris gets there, it will change into a great stadium. The match is nearly over. Chris will go on as a substitute.
	(Chris trots off stage to his right. Blister picks up the ball and stands on a white square)
Blister:	What about me, then? When do I get my turn?
Adam:	Now. What is your wish?
Blister:	The bulldozer. That's what I want.
Narrator:	The bulldozer bursts into life and waves its bucket up and down. Blister waves back.
Adam:	What do you want it to do?
Blister:	**(licking his lips)** I want it to chase people and anything that moves. Just think, we'll scare those ponies to death...
Narrator:	Adam tells Blister to go down to the bulldozer.

This page may be photocopied for use by the purchasing institution only.

Brilliant Publications – Fun with Plays
Saving Blister by Stan Barrett

51

(Blister strides off stage to the right)

Narrator: The bulldozer, still waving its bucket, comes to meet Blister. He stops and waits. In this world, time passes quickly.

(Chris rushes on from the right, Tracey from the left. They speak the next two lines together)

Chris: Fantastic! They all laughed when I went on. But you should have heard them cheer when I scored...

Tracey: It was brilliant! I could see for miles. It was like being in heaven. Just drifting along, looking down...

(They stop when they see Blister and the bulldozer down to their right)

Chris:	**(pointing)** What's happening there?
Tracey:	Blister's trying to run away from that bulldozer. It's chasing him!
	(Their eyes follow Blister and the bulldozer from right to left and back again)
Chris:	It'll kill him!
Adam:	This is Blister's wish.
Chris:	What did he want?
Adam:	He wanted the bulldozer to chase people and anything that moves.
Tracey:	And now it's chasing him! Serves him right! But we've got to save him.
Adam:	I cannot undo a wish.
Blister:	**(from off stage)** Help! Help me!
Chris:	Adam! We've got to do something!
	(pause)
Adam:	Blister! Stand still and it won't touch you. It only chases things that move.
Narrator:	But Blister keeps on running. Tracey and Chris gasp when they see him stumble and fall.
Blister:	**(faintly)** Help!
Tracey and Chris:	Blister!
Adam:	Blister! Whatever you do, keep still!
Narrator:	The bulldozer stops with its bucket hanging over Blister. For the moment, he is safe.

Tracey:	I know it's his own fault, but we've got to save him!
Chris:	Yes. Come on, Adam. You got us here. What do we do?
Adam:	This is not really me. It's that birthday card. That's what gives me power.
Tracey:	Then do something!
Adam:	Wait... I'm thinking...
Chris:	**(to Tracey)** The old man in the shop was right. That card - it's magic...
Narrator:	After a moment, Adam tells Chris and Tracey they must find the card. It is in its white envelope and it's lying on one of the white squares. They get down on hands and knees and search... **(pause)** Quite soon, Tracey shouts:
Tracey:	It's here! I can see it!
Adam:	TRACEY! DON'T TOUCH IT!
Tracey:	**(leaping back)** Why not?
Adam:	The only way out of here is by tearing the card up.
Chris:	**(getting to his feet)** Then let's do it.
Adam:	No. Only one person can do it – Blister.
Tracey:	**(wails)** Blister? But Blister can't move! He'll get killed!
	(Pause)
Chris:	Hang on. I've got an idea.
Narrator:	Chris talks quietly to Tracey and keeps pointing at the bulldozer.
Chris:	Adam, I'm going down there to see if I can get the bulldozer to chase me instead of Blister.

Brilliant Publications – Fun with Plays
Saving Blister by Stan Barrett

Tracey:	And then we get Blister up here and he tears up the card.
	(Chris trots off stage to his right)
Adam:	And then we all go home. **(Louder)** Good luck, Chris.
Tracey:	**(wringing her hands as she watches)** I don't like this. Chris says he's a good runner, but... **(Pause)** He's done it! Now the bulldozer's chasing Chris! Run Chris! BLISTER! Up here! Quick!
	(Enter Blister looking dazed)
Adam:	Blister. Pick up the card.
Blister:	Card? What card?
Tracey:	**(pointing to the card)** Look! There!
	(Blister picks up the card)
Adam:	Blister. Tear the card into little pieces and throw them away.
Narrator:	Blister looks baffled, but does as he is told.
Tracey:	Look! Look at the scenery! It's... It's melting!
Adam:	Go back through the door in the wall. Quick! Before it disappears.
Narrator:	Blister rushes to the door, but pauses when he sees that Tracey is waiting.
Tracey:	Chris! Chris! Run up here! We're going back through the door.
Blister:	Come on, Chris! Run!
	(Enter Chris from the right. He looks shattered, but rushes to the door. The three actors freeze in the doorway for a moment, then turn round. It is as if they have stepped back into the real world)

This page may be photocopied for use by the purchasing institution only.

Brilliant Publications – Fun with Plays
Saving Blister by Stan Barrett

55

(Enter Adam from their left)

Chris: Here's Adam.

Adam: **(in his normal voice)** Hello. I'm glad you could come.

Blister: You three! You just saved my life. I don't know what to... what to...

Tracey: Blister! What are you on about?

Blister: You know... That bulldozer. It tried to kill me!

Chris: There's no bulldozer here.

Blister: But you saw it chase me. Then it chased you. Through that door there.

(They all look at the blank wall)

Adam: What door? There's no door there. Never has been.

Narrator: Blister is baffled. He looks at each face in turn. Slowly, he realises that he is the only one who remembers what happened.

Adam: Come on. Follow me. Mum's done a great meal for us. **(As he exits)** We've got a brilliant video. And there's this new computer game...

(They follow Adam off stage)

Narrator: After that, Blister stops bullying people. Nobody knows why. Not even Adam. But Blister knows. And now we know.

Playing Away

by Irene Yates

This play is set in the future, in the year 2199 – and life is very different from the life we know now.

The boys of 2199 are sent back into the past (today). They have a very different view from ours. Their ideas about cars, for example, are totally different. Look for other ways in which their ideas and their lives are not like ours.

You would need only a few sound effects to be able to read this play as a radio play. It should also be quite easy to perform, once you have worked out how to set up the different scenes. How could you make a simple set for the Learning Centre, the inside of the car, the screen with Sabba on it?

Things to talk about:
- Do you think that cars really will be extinct by 2199?
- Give reasons for your opinions
- How do you think people will travel?
- Will people still go to school or will there be other ways of learning?
- What do you think these might be?
- What other differences might there be?

Playing Away

by Irene Yates

Cast:

           Narrator
           Rick
           Dav
           Jan
           Sabba
           Mum

Brilliant Publications – Fun with Plays
Playing Away by Irene Yates

Narrator:	The year is 2199. Rick, Dav and Jan are three boys who learn together. There are no schools in 2199. Only learning groups. Groups of three or four students all meet at their Learning Centre, every day, for Mind Practice. Their Mentor is Sabba – whom they contact by digital technology. They have to work on their own projects and every moon they can have six contacts with Sabba for help. If they need to contact her more than six times, they have to go down a Learning Centre Point, move to a different Centre with a different Mentor, and that is REALLY BAD NEWS! They've been with Sabba all through their education so far, and couldn't bear to have to have someone else.
Rick:	I'm sick of this mind practice. We've been working on this history for weeks now, and it doesn't get any more interesting.
Dav:	Who wants to learn about 200 years ago? Not me, for one. I'm more interested in NOW!
Jan:	Aren't we all? It's not as if it's even INTERESTING! I mean – CARS! Honestly!
Rick:	You'd think they'd have known better really, wouldn't you? Just think how stupid it must have been – racing around like maniacs in tin cans that only did about 70 miles an hour!
Narrator:	The boys find this whole idea pretty funny!
Dav:	Tin cans with WHEELS on them!
Jan:	They must have looked mad! Can you IMAGINE!
Rick:	Well, that's what makes it all so boring – it is so HARD to imagine!
Jan:	Cars – or whatever they called them – were just tin cans with wheels on! Racing all over the place.
Dav:	Parked up everywhere as well. I mean when they were going on the ... what did they call them?

This page may be photocopied for use
by the purchasing institution only.

Brilliant Publications – Fun with Plays
Playing Away by Irene Yates

59

Rick:	Roads. You mean roads. Those are the things the cars went on.
Jan:	All stuck down on the ground!
Dav:	So there they were – these tin can things, going along on the ground – all at the same level, I mean it doesn't make any sense –
Rick:	No wonder they were always crashing into each other!
Jan:	Too many of them, down on the ... what did they call them?
Rick:	Roads. I just told you – roads.
Jan:	Yeah, well. So many of them, down on their old roads, they just kept bumping into each other – one after the other probably.
Dav:	Stupid!
Narrator:	The boys all find this idea really silly. They shake their heads.
Rick:	Then there was the stuff they put in them.
Jan:	Oh yeah, that stuff.
Dav:	What stuff?
Rick:	Don't ask me. I don't know what it was.
Jan:	Oily stuff.
Rick:	Out of the ground.
Dav:	Haven't got a clue. I know, let's get Sabba up, and find out.
Rick:	Do we HAVE to?

Jan:	You know we have to. We can't find any more information on Resource Box. We've got a project to do. Boring or not, it'll be us in trouble if we don't get it done.
Dav:	Might as well get Sabba up. If we just get her to help us, the project will get finished, won't it?
Rick:	Yeah. Then all we have to do is start on the next one.
Jan:	Are we going to get Sabba up or not?
Narrator:	The boys all look at each other reluctantly.
Rick:	It'll be fourth time this moon.
Jan:	Only two more left after that.
Dav:	Yeah, well, we might not need her on the next project.
Narrator:	The boys look at each other, then nod. Rick reaches forward. In front of him on the shelf is a tiny computer card. He picks it up and breathes on it. Immediately on the wall in front of them a screen, lights up. Sabba appears.
Sabba:	Boys. I wasn't expecting you again this moon! Stuck, are you?
Rick:	Well – it's not so much that we're stuck, it's just that... we need a bit of –
Sabba:	– help? Well, that's what I'm here for. What are you on?
Jan:	We're on the history project again.
Sabba:	I don't know why you're having so much trouble with it.
Dav:	It's because it's boring.
Sabba:	You're finding it boring?

This page may be photocopied for use
by the purchasing institution only.

Brilliant Publications – Fun with Plays
Playing Away by Irene Yates

61

Rick: Well, it's all OLD stuff, isn't it?

Sabba: That's what history IS.

Jan: Point is, we can't really see the point of it.

Dav: That's if there is a point to it.

Rick: Which, if there is, we just can't see.

Sabba: Okay, okay! The point about history is, if you don't find out about it, you don't know how you got to be where you are.

Rick: I know how I got to be where I am.

Jan: So do I – and it wasn't by sitting in an old tin can and coming on wheels along a – what do you call it?

Dav: ROAD. He means road. He means he didn't get here by...

Sabba: That's not what I meant. I didn't mean LITERALLY how you got to be here – I meant how the world got to be the world it is today.

Rick: Yeah – but what difference does it make? I mean – here we are – in the year two thousand one hundred and ninety-nine and why do we want to know about those old tin cans? They don't exist any more. They're EXTINCT aren't they?

Sabba: You have to imagine what life was like with them.

Jan: Why? Today we just whip out our solar-mega-trav-boards and transfer. And before we know we've left, we've arrived.

Dav: What could be easier?

Sabba: Yes, but can't you see – if it hadn't been for cars and petrol and pollution and all that –

Dav:	That's it! That's the word! Petrol!
Rick:	Which word?
Dav:	The word we couldn't remember. The one we had to call Sabba up for.
Rick:	Oh yeah. I remember now. It's PETROL!
Jan:	What is?
Rick:	The oily stuff they put in the tin cans.
Dav:	And we've called Sabba up for that. Lost another Mentorlife!
Jan:	Told you. We've only got two left now.
Rick:	Wasn't my fault.
Jan:	It was actually!
Rick:	Well, it wouldn't have happened if they'd used solar power. We wouldn't have forgotten THAT, would we?
Dav:	Yes, but that's MODERN, isn't it? They didn't know about it then.
Rick:	I think some of them did. Just a bit. They'd just started...
Sabba:	Boys! Boys! Look – now I'm here –
Narrator:	She waves her arms about on the screen and smiles at them.
Sabba:	Now you've lost another Mentorlife you might as well make it worth your while.
Narrator:	The boys look at each other glumly. Sabba always does this to them. She HATES them to waste their Mentorlives – always tries to give them something else to make the Mentorlife worth while.

Sabba:	Why don't I – why don't I get you a little adventure?
Rick:	**(suspiciously)** What kind of adventure?
Sabba:	An historical one of course.
Jan:	Could we bear it?
Dav:	If it's anything like the last one –
Sabba:	Oh, come on, Dav. I told you that was a mistake. I didn't mean for the ship to sink. You were supposed to get off it before it went down –
Dav:	Yes, but you weren't there to get us off, were you? And before we knew what was happening –
Jan:	We'd drowned.
Sabba:	I said I was sorry.
Rick:	Yes – but have you any idea what it is like to drown? Have you – really?
Sabba:	'Course I have. I'm a Mentor, aren't I? Can't be a Mentor unless you've been everywhere, done everything. I tell you – I have been places you could not imagine in your wildest dreams –
Rick:	Yeah, yeah.
Sabba:	Anyway – what about it? It would make the mind practice less boring – because you would be IN it. You would be learning about history AS IT HAPPENED instead of just trying to IMAGINE it.
Narrator:	Again, the boys look at each other. They know when Sabba has set her heart on something, they don't stand a chance.
Jan:	Oh, go on then.
Dav:	What have we got to lose?

Rick: Who knows?

Narrator: Sabba laughs and lets her hands dance wildly in the air.

Sabba: Okay – into your virt-seats, boys. And get ready to meet – oh, I know, I've got somebody nice for you today. She's a mum –

Rick: What's a mum?

Sabba: Oh, come on Rick, we've been through this stacks of times. You don't need me to tell you what a mum is.

Jan: Somebody you live with.

Dav: Somebody who looks after you.

Rick: Oh, I remember – somebody who thinks you're wonderful!

Narrator: The boys all laugh at this again. They cannot imagine living the way they've learned the boys – and girls – of the 1900s lived. What they've learned before is that on the whole they lived with families – some of them had a mum and a dad to look after them and think they were wonderful. Others had a mum or maybe a dad. Some had a mum and two dads at different times, or even the other way around. The boys think it's all pretty creepy. They much prefer their own modern version of living where everybody lives together and all the young people are cared for by ALL the adults, and nobody BELONGS particularly to anyone else.

Sabba: Come on, boys. Concentrate. You'll be getting this mum. And you'll be three brothers.

Jan: BROTHERS! What's BROTHERS?

Sabba: (patiently) It means you're all related. You have the same mum and dad. You belong together. You live together.

This page may be photocopied for use by the purchasing institution only.

Brilliant Publications – Fun with Plays
Playing Away by Irene Yates

65

Narrator: The boys think this is hilarious. They understand about everyone being related, because that is fundamental to the human race. But they can't understand that having the same mum and dad means you belong together and live together.

Rick: Bi-zarre!

Jan: Truly bi-zarre!

Dav: Wonder bizarre!

Sabba: I'm sending you back to the year 1999. You're going to be three boys. With their mum. In the car. Going to school. Are you ready?

Narrator: The boys look reluctant. They don't feel too happy about this. Sometimes Sabba's mindpractice simulations go badly wrong. But they more or less have to do what their Mentor tells them. They settle down into their virt-seats and close their eyes.

Sabba: **(her hands dance slowly and rhythmically across the screen)** Settle yourselves down. Think space. Think time. Think... nothing! Black. Void. Negative. Negative. Negative. And – **(she clicks her fingers)**

Brilliant Publications – Fun with Plays
Playing Away by Irene Yates

Narrator:	Immediately the three boys are plunged back into the past. They find themselves in a house, getting ready for school. It's dark and raining outside, and they're late...
Mum:	Come on, boys! Aren't you ready yet? Ricky – where are your shoes?
Rick:	Shoes? I don't know what shoes are.
Mum:	Don't mess about. Please don't make me late this morning... Which of you two has got Rick's shoes? Give them back to him and let's get on – purlease!
Narrator:	Jan and Dav laugh. Then they find a pair of shoes and pass them to Rick.
Jan:	You don't half look funny! You've got some funny clothes on!
Rick:	So have you two!
Mum:	I'm going to start the car. Get a move on! I want you ready when I pip the horn.
Narrator:	The boys double up with laughter.
Jan:	Pip the horn? What does that mean?
Dav:	Your guess is as good as mine!
Rick:	Come and help me with these SHOES!
Narrator:	At last the boys are ready – JUST in time!
Mum:	**(appearing at front door)** Come on! Didn't you hear me pipping you? Oh never mind, just hurry up – you're going to be late for school. Dave have you put a comb through your hair this morning? It doesn't look like it! John – put your tie straight. That's better. Now then. Packed lunches.
Narrator:	The mum gives them each a plastic box. The boys look at them wondering what on earth they are.

Mum:	Favourite biscuits this morning, boys. But don't get eating them till breaktime.
Narrator:	The boys wonder what on earth 'favourite biscuits' are, but their mum hurries them into the car, Dav and Jan in the back, Rick in the front because he's the oldest.
Mum:	Come on. Fasten your seatbelts.
Rick:	Don't know how to.
Mum:	Ricky, I wish you wouldn't play silly games when we're late.
Narrator:	She leans over, pulls Rick's seat belt around him and fastens it. In the back, Jan and Dav are just sitting there, grinning, so she jumps out of the car, runs round to the back, opens the doors and leans over and fastens them both in, too.
Mum:	Oh boys. Sometimes you are so silly.
Narrator:	Mum starts up the car. The boys begin to grin. They can't believe that they are really going to do this – really going to travel in a tin can, propelled by oily stuff, on the ground.
Mum:	Lot of traffic this morning.
Rick:	That's true.
Jan:	Look at it. I can't believe it. Tin cans everywhere.
Dav:	Hundreds of them.
Mum:	Well, it's rush-hour. But it IS worse this morning. I'll give you that. It must be the weather.
Rick:	I can't see where I'm going.
Mum:	I've got the windscreen wipers on as fast as I can.

Jan:	But it's not fast enough. Look, the rain's hitting the window so fast, the wipers aren't getting rid of it, it's just making it worse.
Mum:	Don't be silly, John. I can't make them go any faster.
Dav:	Well no, they wouldn't go any faster, would they? But that's not the point. The point is – they don't do the job they're meant to do.
Mum:	Oh Dave – don't start. Sometimes you sound just like your dad. He's always going on about things not being efficient enough.
Dav:	Well they're not, are they. I mean, the rain's coming down THIS fast, and the windscreen wipers are going THIS fast, and the two don't meet, so what's the point...
Mum:	Oh Dave, please shut up, it's hard enough trying to drive through this weather, without you keeping on.
Narrator:	Suddenly there's a loud hooting right behind them. The boys nearly jump out of their skin.
Mum:	It's all right. It's only somebody trying to make me go faster. Well, I'm not going faster. Nobody's going to make me go faster, not in this weather.
Jan:	The point is – nobody should be going faster, should they? In fact they shouldn't be going. Not in this weather. Not in a tin can. I mean – we wouldn't go, would we, not even on our S.M.T.B.'s.
Mum:	On your what?
Rick:	It's all right, Mum – it's just something he's been doing at school.
Dav:	A project. A history project.
Mum:	Oh.
Rick:	That's right. Isn't it... er, JOHN? A history project.

This page may be photocopied for use by the purchasing institution only.

Brilliant Publications – Fun with Plays
Playing Away by Irene Yates

69

Jan:	Yeah, but...
Rick:	Jan – shut up! Just let Mum drive the car.
Mum:	Anyway – I've GOT to go to work. And you've GOT to go to school.
Jan:	Why?
Mum:	Because you have to, that's all.
Jan:	But we don't –
Rick:	Ssssh!
Dav:	**(warning)** Oh, be quiet... er, John! I know – open your box and see what your favourite biscuit is.
Mum:	I told you they're for breaktime.
Dav:	Yes, but...
Mum:	If you eat them now, you'll have to go without...
Narrator:	The three boys all dive into their boxes. They each find a chunky chocolate biscuit bar. Not quite sure what to do with them, Rick tears the wrapper off his first and takes a bite.
Rick:	**(savouring the biscuit)** Wow! This is really great!
Mum:	**(laughing)** Honestly, Ricky, sometimes I wonder about you!
Narrator:	The other two bite into their biscuits too. They cannot believe the taste. They've only ever swallowed capsules before: they haven't a clue about chocolate and biscuit.
Jan:	Oh, this is absolutely megabrill.
Dav:	Absolutely.

Rick:	Have you got any more?
Mum:	There are some more in the biscuit tin and then that's the end till I get paid again. Now for goodness' sake let me concentrate on my driving –
Narrator:	The boys all look at each other and laugh.
Rick:	I can't believe we're really doing this!
Jan:	Sitting in a tin can –
Dav:	Bowling along on the ground –
Narrator:	And as they're all grinning at each other there comes the most terrible squeal of brakes and a huge and thunderous crash as an articulated lorry swings across the road and collides with them.
Mum:	**(screaming)** Boys! Oh Boys! My babies! My babies!
Narrator:	Later, Rick, Jan and Dav are telling Sabba all about it.
Rick:	Lights everywhere. Sirens. Rain lashing down.
Jan:	Crashed cars. People crying and sobbing.
Dav:	It was horrible. Horrible.
Rick:	Then these kind of rescuers – I think they were called firefighters – came and they were opening up these tin cans with all kinds of equipment, burning the metal –
Jan:	Oh the stink of it!
Dav:	And people were still moaning and crying.
Rick:	No wonder they got rid of them.
Sabba:	Got rid of them?
Rick:	The tin cans. The cars.

Dav:	Absolutely ridiculous. I could see they didn't work. Even from where I was, in the back. You could see there were too many of them.
Jan:	And they were going too fast.
Rick:	The windscreen wipers were useless.
Dav:	What I couldn't get over was why people thought they HAD to go out in that weather.
Jan:	That's right. I mean, the mum said it, didn't she? She said 'I HAVE to go to work. And you HAVE to go to school.' And I thought – why didn't they just have mindgroups, like ours and mind practice and all that.
Dav:	And what was the work for, anyway? I mean was it to pay for the car, that we were in that raced along, that caused her to die? Or what?
Rick:	She did die, didn't she, Sabba?
Sabba:	I'm afraid she did, Rick. So did her three boys actually.
Jan:	All of them?
Sabba:	I'm sorry to say, they did.
Dav:	And their dad was left all on his own?
Sabba:	Yes, he was.
Rick:	He was probably one of the ones that campaigned to get rid of the tin cans.
Sabba:	Could have been.
Jan:	And that oily stuff. When the crash happened it was all over the – erm...
Dav:	The road.

Jan:	Yes, that's it, the road. It was all over the road.
Rick:	Spilled out of the tanks.
Jan:	And then it set on fire.
Rick:	You can't believe it, really. Can you?
Jan:	I mean, it was only two hundred years ago. A blink of an eye really.
Dav:	I know. And yet it was –
Rick:	– barbaric.
Jan:	Yes. That's the word. Barbaric. As if they knew no better.
Dav:	Well, they didn't, did they?
Rick:	Couldn't have done. **(Pause)** Thank goodness for solar power.
Narrator:	The boys all nod, satisfied with what they've learned. Sabba's happy too.
Sabba:	Well your fourth contact this moon wasn't completely wasted, was it? You got something out of it.
Rick:	Well, yes, I suppose so. I'll tell you something else –
Jan:	What?
Rick:	That Mum was okay really, wasn't she? I mean – I can see why they liked living like that – in sort of little houses – together – you know what I mean?
Dav:	Being with a mum and dad?
Rick:	Yeah. It was kind of nice – having somebody –
Jan:	All of your own.

Narrator: Sabba laughs and her image on the screen slowly gets smaller and smaller until it vanishes. Rick stretches forward and breathes onto his computer card. The boys all sigh in unison.

Dav: A bit like Sabba really. With us.

Narrator: The boys all think about it. But before they get too serious –

Rick: I'll tell you something else.

Dav: What's that then?

Jan: I bet I know what you're going to say...

Rick: That chocolate biscuit – beats a food capsule any day...

Back Chat

by Trevor Harvey

This play tells the kind of thing that happens in classrooms all the time. Poor David thinks he's always in trouble – and it's not his fault. Poor Miss Watts has her work cut out, trying to keep her pupils in order. You should read it out with lots of pace to make it fun. The characters don't have to be wearing trainers with velcro on them, you could HAVE a props assistant standing to one side, making the sound effects with just one pair of trainers.

In fact, if you wanted to perform to an audience, the play would make a good radio play because of its sound effects. You would need to go through the script, marking up all the sound effects you could find – including people moving chairs and places, doors opening, etc. One person takes charge of making all the sound effects. The whole group stand around the microphone, or cassette recorder, to read and record. The sound effects person makes the sounds as they appear in the script.

Things to talk about:

- What do you like about this script?
- How would you describe it?
- How difficult is it to settle into a new classroom when everybody else knows one another and you've just come in new in the middle of term?
- Do you think it's as hard for a teacher as a pupil?
- Why do you think the children are giving Miss Watts such a hard time?

Back Chat

by Trevor Harvey

Cast:

Narrator
David (a new pupil)
Rashid
Mary
Jamie
Miss Watts

Narrator:	It is the start of the school day. 5W are in their classroom. It's the second week of term. Their teacher, Miss Watts, is standing outside the classroom door. She is talking to a parent in the school corridor. The children are busy chatting to each other as they wait for her to come into the room.
Rashid:	What's wrong, David? Don't you feel well?
David:	**(sighs)** I'm O.K.
Mary:	He's sulking. My sister sulks. She doesn't talk to anyone for DAYS!
Rashid:	I don't blame her. If you were MY sister, I think I'd sulk as well!
Mary:	**(Mary 'pulls a face' at Rashid, then turns to David)** You ARE sulking, aren't you, David?
David:	No.
Mary:	What's wrong, then?
David:	This school – THAT'S what's wrong!
Mary:	You've only been here TWO DAYS!
David:	I liked my old school better. Since I moved here, I've always been in trouble!
Rashid:	It's your own fault!
David:	It isn't! Miss Watts keeps picking on me. I get blamed for EVERYTHING.
Rashid:	She tells you off because you keep talking.
David:	I DON'T keep talking!
Rashid:	Yes you do!
David:	No. I don't.

This page may be photocopied for use by the purchasing institution only.

Brilliant Publications – Fun with Plays
Back Chat by Trevor Harvey

77

Rashid:	Well, if it's not you who's talking, who is it then?
David:	I don't tell on people.
Mary:	I bet it's JAMIE!
Rashid:	Is it?
David:	I'm not saying.
Mary:	See? I told you! It IS Jamie. I've seen him. He hides behind his book and laughs each time David gets told off.
Rashid:	That's not fair. Why doesn't Miss Watts tell Jamie off as well?
Mary:	She knows his mum. I saw them shopping together on Saturday.
Rashid:	Teachers shouldn't have favourites.
Mary:	She's a new teacher. Miss Watts wasn't here last year, David.
Rashid:	That's right. You're not the only new person at this school.
Mary:	My mum wants me to help Miss Watts. She says I've got to be 'really kind'.
Rashid:	Miss Watts isn't kind to US! The work she gives us is REALLY hard. Jamie is the only person who can get it right.
David:	I get it right as well.
Rashid:	That's because you sit next to Jamie. I'm sure I'd get all my work right if I sat there.
David:	That's not true!
Rashid:	It is! I'm very good at copying!

 Brilliant Publications – Fun with Plays
Back Chat by Trevor Harvey

David:	I don't copy Jamie's work. Jamie copies MINE!
Rashid:	**(not believing him)** Oh yeah...?
David:	**(annoyed)** Yeah!
Mary:	I've got an idea.
Rashid:	Don't faint, everyone! Mary's got an idea. It must be the first time THAT'S happened in YEARS.
Mary:	If David keeps getting blamed for things that aren't his fault, why doesn't he move to a different seat?
Rashid:	Smart thinking!
David:	Miss Watts will tell me off for moving!
Mary:	She won't. I don't think she'll even notice.
David:	Are you sure?
Mary:	It's worth a try.
Rashid:	You've got a seat at the BACK of the class, haven't you, David?
David:	Yes.
Rashid:	Then why don't we change places?
Mary:	Great! You sit at Rashid's table – and he'll sit at yours.
Rashid:	Say yes, David. I've always wanted to sit at the back of the class.
David:	Oh – all right, then. I'll give it a try.
Narrator:	David and Rashid move to each other's seat. Miss Watts says goodbye to the parent, opens the door and comes into the classroom.
Miss Watts:	Good morning, everyone.

All:	Good morning, Miss Watts.
Miss Watts:	David! Who said you could move to a different seat?
David:	See? I told you what she'd say!
Miss Watts:	Have you swopped with Rashid? Go back to your proper seats AT ONCE!
Narrator:	David and Rashid do as Miss Watts tells them. Jamie arrives with the class register. He gives it to Miss Watts.
Miss Watts:	Thank you, Jamie. Sit down, please. Listen, everyone. We have whole school assembly after break this morning. I want you all to be on your BEST behaviour. Yesterday, I'm sure I heard a couple of people playing with the velcro on their trainers. You all know what I mean, DON'T YOU?
All:	Yes, Miss.
Mary:	It's doing this, isn't it, Miss?
Narrator:	Mary pulls back the velcro on her left trainer. It makes a loud noise. Miss Watts is NOT very pleased!
Miss Watts:	Are you trying to be CHEEKY, Mary?
Mary:	No, Miss. I'm trying to be HELPFUL.
Miss Watts:	As I was saying, if I hear ANY velcro noises at this morning's assembly, I shall keep the whole class in at lunchtime.
Rashid:	Then you can have each of us do a velcro noise in turn, Miss, until you find out who it was!
Mary:	Yeah. Shall we do it for you now, Miss?
Narrator:	Mary pulls the velcro back again – and Rashid joins in as well.
Miss Watts:	That's enough, Mary! Thank you, Rashid – I can do WITHOUT your help.

Narrator:	Miss Watts turns to write the date on the whiteboard. There are ten sums on the board already.
Miss Watts:	I want you ALL to take out your rough books – QUIETLY! – and see how many of these sums you can do while I mark the register.
Narrator:	The children take out their rough books and begin to work. Someone starts talking, so Miss Watts isn't very pleased again.
Miss Watts:	Is that talking I can hear? What do I want to hear instead?
Mary:	Velcro, Miss?
Miss Watts:	No, Mary! I want to hear SILENCE. The noise seems to be coming from the back table again. Is there a problem, Jamie?
Jamie:	No, Miss.
Mary:	There IS, Miss!
Miss Watts:	You're not sitting at the back table, Mary.
Mary:	No, Miss – but I saw what happened. It WAS Jamie.
Jamie:	It wasn't!
Mary:	He punched David.
Jamie:	I didn't!
Mary:	You did!
Jamie:	I gave him a prod, that's all. To make him get on with his work, Miss.
Miss Watts:	Well, don't touch David in future, please. But it's good to know that SOMEONE in this class is thinking about work, Jamie.

Rashid:	I think about it a lot, Miss!
Miss Watts:	Then it's a pity YOU don't DO it. And David –
David:	I haven't done anything, Miss!
Miss Watts:	That's the trouble. I think you're disturbing a hard-working table. It might be better if I moved you, after all.
Jamie:	I don't mind helping him with his work, Miss.
Miss Watts:	That's kind of you, Jamie, but David has to learn to work on his own. David, you can move to Mary's seat – and Mary can sit next to Jamie.
Mary:	Oooh, Miss!
Narrator:	Mary is not happy about this, but it's clear Miss Watts is NOT going to change her mind – so she and David change places.
Miss Watts:	That's enough fuss, Mary – and I hope YOU won't copy Jamie's work, will you?
David:	I never copied Jamie's work, either, Miss! He copied MINE.
Jamie:	No, I didn't!
Miss Watts:	We'll say no more about it. I've only just moved you to a new table, David, but you're already causing a disturbance!
Jamie:	I expect he was the one who made the noises yesterday, Miss.
Miss Watts:	The noises...?
Jamie:	With the velcro – like this, Miss.
Narrator:	Jamie pulls back the velcro from his left shoe.

Miss Watts:	Quite likely. Now, I want you all to get on with your work. I shall never get the register marked if I have any more interruptions.
Narrator:	Miss Watts starts to mark the class register. Suddenly she hears voices from the back of the room again.
Miss Watts:	David – is that you talking at the back of the classroom?
David:	No, Miss – you moved me to the middle table.
Miss Watts:	Perhaps it would be better if you sat at the FRONT of the class, where I can see you. I think Mary is causing a problem at the back table now. Rashid, will you move from the front table, please, and sit where Mary is sitting? Mary, will you move back to your old seat – and David, will you come to the place where Rashid was sitting? Is that clear?
All:	Yes, Miss.
Miss Watts:	Then do it QUIETLY!
Narrator:	They change seats again – but Rashid and Mary end up at the same chair.
Rashid:	Please, Miss – there are TWO of us at this seat!
Miss Watts:	You weren't paying attention, Rashid! Use your eyes! Look to see where there's an empty chair!
Mary:	We play this game at birthday parties, Miss.
Miss Watts:	Are you being cheeky again, Mary?
Mary:	No, Miss.
Narrator:	Rashid finds his place and sits down at last.
Miss Watts:	Now – I want to see EVERYONE working. I expect Jamie is the only person who has finished the sums that I've put on the board.

Mary:	He hasn't even STARTED, Miss – well, he hadn't when I was sitting next to him a minute ago!
Miss Watts:	Is that TRUE, Jamie?
Jamie:	It's been too noisy, Miss. The class has stopped me from working.
Miss Watts:	It HAS been noisy this morning – hasn't it?
All:	Yes, Miss...
Miss Watts:	David, why are you sitting and staring into space?
David:	I've finished, Miss.
Miss Watts:	FINISHED? I don't believe it! Bring me your book!
Narrator:	David takes his book to Miss Watts. She is amazed! She puts a TICK by each of the sums. He's got everything RIGHT!
Miss Watts:	I can't believe it! How on EARTH did you manage to do so well?
Jamie:	He copied me.
Rashid:	He can't have done, Miss! He's been sitting in a different seat.
Jamie:	He copied me before he moved.
Rashid:	Jamie hasn't even STARTED yet!
Miss Watts:	Well, Jamie...?
Jamie:	He – he must have copied me before I'd written them down!
Miss Watts:	Jamie – I DO hope you're not being SILLY...!
Jamie:	No, Miss.

Brilliant Publications – Fun with Plays
Back Chat by Trevor Harvey

Miss Watts:	Well done, David. You seem to be working well now you are sitting at the front of the class. Perhaps you had better stay there. I hope the improvement continues.
David:	Yes, Miss Watts.
Narrator:	David goes back to his seat.
Miss Watts:	Listen, everyone – I've something important to tell you. When you see me after lunch, I may look different.
Rashid:	Wow! Are you turning into a werewolf, Miss?
Miss Watts:	Don't be so silly, Rashid. I'm going to the opticians to collect a pair of glasses.
Mary:	You don't wear glasses, Miss.
Miss Watts:	I shall be from now on. It's because I'm short-sighted.
Mary:	You look quite tall, Miss.
Miss Watts:	**(crossly)** Mary...!
Mary:	Sorry, Miss...
Miss Watts:	When I wear my glasses, I shall be able to see right to the back of the classroom. I shall be able to see who is busy talking and who is busy working. So that will be good – won't it, Jamie?
Jamie:	**(sadly)** Yes, Miss...
David:	GREAT!
Narrator:	Suddenly, there is a loud noise, as if two strips of velcro are being pulled back at once.
Miss Watts:	JAMIE!
Jamie:	Yes, Miss...?

This page may be photocopied for use
by the purchasing institution only.

Brilliant Publications – Fun with Plays
Back Chat by Trevor Harvey

85

Miss Watts: Have YOU just pulled back the velcro on your trainers?

Narrator: All the class look at Jamie, then point at him and shout:

All: YES, MISS!

                         **(Everybody pulls back the velcro on their shoes at
                         the same time, making a loud ending to the playlet)**

Aladdin and the Magic Lamp

adapted by Moira Andrew

This play is not the pantomime version of Aladdin which you may be familiar with. It is adapted from a Chinese legend and tells a very serious tale.

At its heart is a message about greed and need – it is up to you to work out what the legend teaches you. After you have read the play through a couple of times, have a discussion about it and see what answers you can come up with.

There are several scenes in the play and you may need to find a way of introducing each scene and making it cut off from the preceding and following scenes. For instance, you may have a 'voice off' which introduces a scene, or you may have a piece of music or a sound symbol to do so.

Things to talk about:
- What do you think about Aladdin's willingness to strike up a conversation with the 'Uncle'?
- When did you first suspect a trick and what made you suspect it?
- Do you think Aladdin should have done something different or not – if so, what?
- Because Aladdin 'wins' in the end, do you think it means that everything was all right after all?
- Can you make any moral judgements on the characters' actions in the play?

Aladdin and the Magic Lamp

adapted by Moira Andrew

Cast: **Storyteller** **Witch of the Trees**
Aladdin **Genie of the Ring**
Mother **Genie of the Lamp**
Stranger/Uncle **Emperor**
Gold Wizard **Princess**
Silver Wizard
Stall-holders, shoppers and courtiers

Brilliant Publications – Fun with Plays
Aladdin and the Magic Lamp adapted by Moira Andrew

Storyteller:	This legend from ancient China tells the story of Aladdin and his magic lamp. When Aladdin was a baby, his father died so he and his mother lived alone in a little house in the hills. They never had enough money, although Aladdin's mother worked very hard, washing and ironing all day for the rich people who lived in big houses in the town.

Scene 1:	**Inside Aladdin's house. There is wet washing hanging all around, a tub of water on the floor and an old-fashioned iron ready for use.**

Mother:	(shouting) Aladdin! Aladdin! Where is that boy? **(She goes to the door and looks out)** Aladdin!
Aladdin:	**(not to be seen, only his voice)** I'm off to the market, Mother. I promise I won't be long.
Mother:	My poor aching back! I must empty this tub of dirty water and it's so heavy. I wish Aladdin had stayed to help me. **(She lifts the heavy tub and takes it to the door)** But I mustn't grumble – he's a good boy at heart! I expect he will bring back something good for supper.

Scene 2:	**A busy marketplace with stall-holders noisily selling their wares.**

Stall-holders: (optional)	Buy my fresh fish! Buy my ripe fruit! Buy rich silks from foreign lands! Come and buy! Come and buy!
Storyteller:	Aladdin strolls through the crowds, stopping to look with interest at all the people buying and selling. He stops at the fish stall.
Aladdin:	My mother would like a fine fresh fish for supper. I wonder how much it costs. What? Oh, too much, too much! I haven't got enough money! **(He walks away, not noticing a stranger coming up behind him. The stranger taps Aladdin on the shoulder)**

This page may be photocopied for use by the purchasing institution only.

Brilliant Publications – Fun with Plays
Aladdin and the Magic Lamp adapted by Moira Andrew

89

Stranger:	I couldn't help hearing what you said, my boy. Please let me buy a few fish for your mother. I have lots of money. **(He pulls out gold coins from his pocket)**
Aladdin:	Thank you very much, sir. But no. My mother wouldn't like a stranger to buy our supper. **(Aladdin turns to walk away)**
Stranger:	Turn round, lad, and let me have a good look at you. **(He looks intently at Aladdin)** I thought as much! You are the image of my long-lost brother. Your must take me to meet your father.
Aladdin:	Sir, my father is dead. I live alone with my mother.
Stranger:	You must forgive me, my boy. I travel far and wide and I didn't know your father had died. What is your name boy? I've forgotton.
Aladdin:	Aladdin, sir.
Stranger:	Yes, yes, of course, a good Chinese name. And you've got my brother's dark eyes! You even sound like him.
Aladdin:	That's strange. I didn't know that my father had a brother. I've never heard him talk about you.
Stranger:	Perhaps you were too young to remember! Well, I am your uncle, so you must let me pay for your supper. Here, take this! **(He drops some gold coins into Aladdin's hand)**
Aladdin:	Thank you, thank you, kind sir.
Stranger:	Don't say 'sir', Aladdin. Not any more. Remember, I'm your uncle now. Show me where you live. I will come this evening to meet my sister-in-law. Good-bye till then.
Aladdin:	Good-bye, Uncle. I'll tell my mother you are coming. I'm sure she will look foward to meeting you.
	(The stranger goes off with a wave and Aladdin stares with delight at the gold coins)

Brilliant Publications – Fun with Plays
Aladdin and the Magic Lamp adapted by Moira Andrew

Storyteller:	Aladdin had never seen so much money. He went round the market stalls buying as much food as he could carry. Then he rushed off home to tell his mother the exciting news.

Scene 3:	**Inside Aladdin's house.**

Aladdin:	**(shouting)** Mother! Mother! Guess what? I met my uncle in the marketplace and...
Mother:	Your uncle? But, Aladdin, you haven't got an uncle!
Aladdin:	Well, I have now. He says he's Father's brother – and he's very rich. Look, Mother, he gave me lots of gold coins, so I bought pineapples and lemons and fish and rice and...
Mother:	Stop! Stop! What will we do with all this food? It's more than we usually have in a month.
Aladdin:	I forgot to tell you, Mother. My new uncle is coming for supper tonight.
Mother:	Oh, my goodness! We had better get on. Aladdin, help me tidy up. We must make ready for our visitor.
Storyteller:	Aladdin and his mother scurried around cleaning and tidying their little house until there wasn't a speck of dust to be seen and every window shone like the sun. Then they dressed in their best clothes, old and patched to be sure, but all clean and freshly ironed.
	(There is a loud knock on the door. Aladdin goes to open it and shows the stranger into the house. The stranger is richly dressed in coloured silks and jewels. He wears a turban on his head)
Aladdin:	Come in, Uncle. This is my mother. **(The stranger bows to Aladdin's mother)**
Uncle:	I'm so pleased to meet you, dear lady, after all this time. My dear brother told me all about you. I was so sorry to hear that he had died while I was on my travels.

This page may be photocopied for use
by the purchasing institution only.

Brilliant Publications – Fun with Plays
Aladdin and the Magic Lamp adapted by Moira Andrew

91

Mother: Welcome to our home, kind sir. But I'm puzzled my husband never told me he had a brother!

Uncle: Aren't people strange? Well, we can't ask my brother any questions now, so I'll tell what I have in mind for young Aladdin here!

Aladdin: For me, Uncle? But you don't know anything about me!

Uncle: Perhaps not, but I like what I see. I have no child of my own, so I'm going to make you my heir. When you have finished school, I will teach you to be a merchant. What do you think about that, Sister-in-law?

Mother: I will miss my son, but I won't stand in his way.

Aladdin: I think it will be wonderful!

Uncle: But first, I'd like to buy you some new clothes. I can't have my heir going round in rags! What would my friends think?

Storyteller: After supper, Aladdin kissed his mother good-bye and went off with his uncle into the night. He was very excited. Next day, the pair went round the market and Aladdin was introduced to all the merchants as a long-lost nephew. Aladdin's uncle bought him rich presents and lots of new clothes. He could hardly believe his luck.

Scene 4:	The marketplace.

Aladdin: It's beginning to get dark, Uncle. Mother will be worried about me, so I must get back home. Thank you for all my presents. You are very kind. **(Yawns)** I'll see you in the morning, Uncle.

Uncle: Don't go yet, boy. I'd like to go for a walk to get some country air into my lungs before bedtime. Come along.

Aladdin: But Uncle...

Uncle: Grow up, lad. It's not bedtime yet!

92 **Brilliant Publications – Fun with Plays**
Aladdin and the Magic Lamp adapted by Moira Andrew

This page may be photocopied for use by the purchasing institution only.

Storyteller:	So Aladdin went off with his uncle. They walked and walked, deep into the countryside. When Aladdin looked back, he saw that the town seemed far away and the hill where his own little house stood couldn't be seen at all.

Scene 5: **On a deserted path, far from the town.**

Uncle:	I'm getting rather cold. I think we should build a fire. Bring me some twigs and sticks, Nephew!
Aladdin:	But Uncle, I want to go home. My mother will be frantic with worry!
Uncle:	You are a big boy now, Aladdin. Do as I say! Quickly!
Storyteller:	So Aladdin gathered a pile of twigs and took them back to where his uncle was sitting by the path. The man stood up and threw a handful of dust on to the dry sticks. All at once there was a roar like a volcano and red-hot flames leapt from a white-hot fire. Aladdin's uncle danced round the fire. He began to mutter strange words and wave his hands over the flames. Suddenly, as quickly as it had taken hold, the fire died down. As the smoke cleared, among the ashes, Aladdin saw a trap-door with a heavy metal ring in the middle. He saw his uncle stare at him in a very strange way.
Aladdin:	What has happened, Uncle? Is anything wrong?
Uncle:	**(in a fierce voice)** Stupid boy! You don't really think I'm your uncle! I have pretended to be your uncle so that you would be willing to come here with me. Do you see the trap-door?
Aladdin:	**(in a small frightened voice)** Yes, Uncle.
Uncle:	You are going to open that trap-door and go down deep into the heart of the earth. There you will find riches beyond your wildest dreams.
Aladdin:	Why me? Why don't you go, Uncle'?

Brilliant Publications – Fun with Plays
Aladdin and the Magic Lamp adapted by Moira Andrew

Uncle: Because the Guardians of the Underworld live there. They will work their wicked magic on me if I as much as touch that metal ring.

Aladdin: But what about me?

Uncle: (laughing heartily) They won't harm a young boy like you. I promise you, they're not as wicked as that!

Storyteller: Aladdin looked round, hoping to escape, but his uncle cruelly twisted his arm and made him grab the brass ring and pull open the heavy door. Inside was a deep dark hole with steps going far down into the darkness.

Uncle: All I ask is that you bring me an old brass lamp that the Guardians of the Underworld have hidden from me. Any jewels you find, you can keep. That's fair, boy, isn't it?

Aladdin: But Uncle, I'm frightened. It looks very dark and spooky down there.

Uncle: Not to worry, boy. I'll give you this magic ring to protect you. Now, off you go!

Storyteller: And he gave Aladdin such a hefty push that he tumbled down a steep staircase into the depths of a echoing cave. He picked himself up and looked about him. Fireflies, twinkling like little white stars, lit up the darkness. In the gloom, Aladdin could just make out great bags full of silver coins. He tiptoed across to an open bag. All at once, an old man appeared. He was wearing a silver suit.

Scene 6:	**Inside the caves, deep in the heart of the earth. It is almost dark. Bags full of coins lie on the floor.**

Silver Wizard: Stop, boy! I am the guardian of the silver cave. If you touch just one silver coin I will change you into a mouse!

Brilliant Publications – Fun with Plays
Aladdin and the Magic Lamp adapted by Moira Andrew

Aladdin: Please sir, I don't intend to steal your money. I'm looking for my uncle's old brass lamp. He said you might have it here.

Silver Wizard: Not me, boy. Try further on where my brother, the Gold Wizard, keeps his gold.

Storyteller: So Aladdin went on to another cave. Barrels full of gold lay on the floor. Unseen by Aladdin, an old man in a golden suit was watching his every move.

Aladdin: **(going to look inside the nearest barrel)** Gold! If I had just one of these coins, my mother could rest for a whole week.

Gold Wizard: Stop, boy! I am the guardian of the gold cave. If you touch just one of these golden coins, I will turn you into a toad!

Aladdin:	Please sir, I don't intend to steal your money. I'm looking for my uncle's old brass lamp. He said you might have it.
Storyteller:	So Aladdin went on. He came to an orchard where instead of fruit, jewels – diamonds, rubies and emeralds – hung from every branch of every tree. The orchard was so bright with colour, it was like walking through a rainbow. Unseen by Aladdin, an old woman watched his every move. She wore a flowing cloak of many colours.
Aladdin:	**(looking up at the trees)** Such riches! If I had just a few of these jewels, my mother would never need to work again.
Witch of the Trees:	Stop, boy! I am the guardian of the magic orchard. If you touch just one of these jewels, I will change you into a frog!
Aladdin:	Please lady, I don't intend to steal your jewels. I'm looking for my uncle's old brass lamp. This must be the one. **(He finds a dented rusty lamp and holds it high)**
Witch of the Trees:	The old rascal! He stole that lamp from me! Give it back at once! Look, boy, give your uncle this new one instead. **(She holds out a bright shining lamp)**
Aladdin:	Thank you, kind lady, but my uncle was very clear. It's the old dented brass one he wants.
Witch of the Trees:	**(laughing horribly)** Then you will have to catch me first!
Storyteller:	Aladdin and the old woman chased each other in and out of the trees. As they bumped into the branches, jewels dropped to the ground like falling stars. At last the old woman landed in a heap in the corner. She was so out of breath that she couldn't say her magic words, so Aladdin escaped with the rusty old lamp and

 Brilliant Publications – Fun with Plays
Aladdin and the Magic Lamp adapted by Moira Andrew

Storyteller: cont.	his pockets filled with fallen jewels. He ran past the Gold Wizard. He ran past the Silver Wizard till, at last, he came to the bottom of the staircase. From far above, he heard his uncle's voice.
Uncle:	**(in an echoing voice)** Where is that stupid boy? He's taking for ever! I won't get home 'till morning at this rate.
Aladdin:	**(calling from the bottom of the steps)** Uncle, Uncle! Help me up. I've got the lamp.
Uncle:	Silly fellow! He thinks he's going to be rich. Little does he know that I'm going to shut him away deep in the underworld as soon as I get my hands on that lamp. **(In a sweet voice, as he looks down through the trap door)** Well done, Aladdin. Pass the lamp to me and I'll help you up.
Aladdin:	No fear! You must help me up, Uncle, and then I'll give you the lamp.
Uncle:	The miserable little fellow! Does he think he can play games with me? He's made me hopping mad.
Storyteller:	The wicked uncle was so angry that he danced round the trap-door in a rage, shouting and bellowing. By

Storyteller: cont.	accident, he spilled what was left of the magic dust on the dying fire. Flames shot high into the air and the trap-door and its metal ring disappeared for ever with poor Aladdin trapped deep in the undeworld with only the fireflies for company. Aladdin sat on a stone, feeling cold and miserable. Then he put his hands over his face and cried. But, as he did so, he rubbed the magic ring his uncle had given him. In a flash of light and a puff of smoke, a genie stood before him. He wore a pigtail and spoke in a very loud voice.
Genie of the Ring:	I am the Genie of the Ring. I am ready and willing to do whatever you ask of me, Master.
Aladdin:	I'm so glad to see you, Genie. Please, can you take me home?
Genie of the Ring:	**(bowing)** At once, Master! Anything you desire!
Storyteller:	Immediately Aladdin found himself back in his own bed in his own little house on top of the hill. But the Genie had disappeared. Aladdin felt in his pockets. They were still stuffed full of jewels.

Scene 7:	**Inside Aladdin's house.**
Aladdin:	Mother! Mother! I'm home safe and sound.
Mother:	My dear boy! I've been so worried. What happened?
Aladdin:	I found out that my uncle isn't an uncle after all. He pushed me into the underground caves and locked me in, but I escaped with the help of the Genie of the Ring.
Mother:	Where did you find this old lamp, Aladdin? **(She holds the rusty lamp up to the light)**
Aladdin:	Oh, that old thing! That was what my uncle wanted me to fetch from the caves.
Mother:	Well, I'll put it on a shelf and you can sell it in the marketplace one day.

98 **Brilliant Publications – Fun with Plays**
Aladdin and the Magic Lamp adapted by Moira Andrew

This page may be photocopied for use
by the purchasing institution only.

Storyteller: So they put the old brass lamp high on a shelf and forgot about it. Aladdin and his mother used a few of the precious jewels to buy food and clothes and kept the rest in a box under Aladdin's bed. They had enough money to live on and Aladdin's mother never again needed to wash and iron for the rich people in the big houses in the town. They never saw the wicked uncle again. Time passed and Aladdin grew up into a handsome man. He still liked to visit the marketplace and listen to the cries of the stall-holders. One day when he was there, the Emperor's daughter came to buy silks. She was surrounded by soldiers, but Aladdin managed to catch a glimpse of her. He thought that she was beautiful and ran home to tell his mother all about her.

Aladdin: Mother, I saw the Emperor's daughter in the market-place today. She is the most beautiful girl I have ever seen and I am going to marry her!

Mother: Marry the Princess! You must be out of your mind, Aladdin. What would the Emperor and his daughter want with poor people like us?

Aladdin: Mother, I have a plan. Remember we hid some of the jewels from the magic orchard? I want you to go to the palace and give them to the Emperor. Tell him that I, Aladdin, wish to marry his daughter!

Mother: Just like that! The Emperor will have me beaten for my insolence.

Aladdin: No he won't. When he sees the rich jewels, he will know I am serious. Please try, Mother.

Storyteller: When Aladdin's mother went to the palace with the message from her son, the Emperor was astonished to see the wonderful jewels.

Scene 8:	**The Emperor's palace. It looks very rich with soldiers in uniform and courtiers dressed in satin and lace. The Emperor is sitting on his throne looking down at Aladdin's mother.**

Emperor: These jewels are even more magnificent than any I possess. Your son must really want to marry my daughter! However, I am very fond of her myself, so I must ask him to send more gifts to prove how serious he is.

Storyteller: Aladdin's mother went off home as fast as she could go. She told Aladdin what the Emperor had said. Aladdin rubbed the magic ring and summoned the Genie of the Ring.

Scene 9:	**Inside Aladdin's house.**

Aladdin: Genie of the Ring, you promised to give me anything I wished for. What I want most of all is to marry the Emperor's daughter but he wants me to offer more precious gifts than the jewels from the magic orchard. Please will you help me?

Genie of the Ring: I'm sorry, Master, but your wish is beyond my powers. You will need the Genie of the Lamp. He is more powerful than I am.

Aladdin: Where will I find such a lamp?

Genie of the Ring: Have you forgotten, Master? It's the one you brought from the caves. Rub it, and the Genie of the Lamp will appear.

Aladdin: That old thing! Mother, where is the old rusty lamp? We didn't sell it, did we?

Mother: It is still here somewhere, I'm sure. Now, where did I put it?

Storyteller: Aladdin's mother searched the house until at last she

 Brilliant Publications – Fun with Plays
Aladdin and the Magic Lamp adapted by Moira Andrew

Storyteller: cont.	found the long-forgotten lamp tucked away at the back of a shelf. She gave it to Aladdin who rubbed it, first with his right, then with his left hand. To his surprise, a cloud of smoke appeared and out of the smoke came a huge figure, richly dressed in a turban studded with shining jewels. He bowed to Aladdin and spoke in a loud booming voice.
Genie of the Lamp:	Ask for your heart's desire and I will obey, Master!
Aladdin:	My heart's desire is to take the Emperor's daughter as my wife, so I must ask for riches and gifts fit for a princess.
Genie of the Lamp:	As you wish, Master!
Storyteller:	Soon the poor kitchen was filled with great caskets of the finest jewels, each carried on a velvet cushion by a servant dressed in silks and satins. Aladdin and his mother stared in amazement. Then they put on their best clothes and led the servants in procession to the Emperor's palace. Aladdin hid the magic lamp under his coat.

Scene 10:	**The Emperor's palace. The Emperor and the Princess are sitting side by side on painted thrones.**

Aladdin:	**(bowing to the Emperor)** Your Highness, I have brought gifts for your daughter.
Emperor:	Bring them here at once!
Aladdin:	**(to the servants)** Present my gifts to the Princess!
Storyteller:	The servants carried in the heavy caskets, placed them in front of the thrones, and opened them one by one. The Emperor and the Princess gazed in amazement as rubies and emeralds, diamonds and sapphires, gold necklaces, silver bracelets and jewelled tiaras spilled out at their feet.
Mother:	Now will you agree to the marriage of my son to your daughter, Your Highness?

This page may be photocopied for use by the purchasing institution only.

Brilliant Publications – Fun with Plays
Aladdin and the Magic Lamp adapted by Moira Andrew

101

Emperor: With such rich gifts before me, I can't say no! What do you say, daughter? **(The Princess whispers in her father's ear)** There is only one more condition. My daughter wants a palace for herself as grand as this one.

(He points around the throne room)

Princess: I'd like furniture of fine polished wood, deep carpets and curtains of rainbow silk.

Aladdin: My dearest, you shall have everything your heart desires!

Storyteller: Aladdin took the magic lamp from under his coat, rubbed it and immediately the genie appeared, once more in a cloud of smoke.

Genie of the Lamp: I am at your service, Master. Ask and I will obey!

Aladdin: I want a magnificent marble palace built within the hour! It should be furnished as the Princess desires.

Genie of the Lamp: As you wish, Master!

Storyteller: Later, when the Princess went to the window, she was astonished to see a beautiful marble palace outside, its white walls shining in the sun. She clapped her hands in delight.

Princess: Thank you, thank you, Aladdin. This is exactly what I wanted!

Mother: **(to the Emperor)** Your daughter seems very happy, Your Highness. Now do you agree to the marriage of my son to your daughter?

Emperor: I am delighted to give my permission.

Aladdin: **(kneeling in front of the Princess)** Princess, please will you marry me? I will love you and take care of you all of our days.

Princess. Yes, Aladdin. I would love to be your wife.

 Brilliant Publications – Fun with Plays
Aladdin and the Magic Lamp adapted by Moira Andrew

Emperor: (puts his daughter's hand into Aladdin's) I hope that you will both be very happy together. Now we must make preparations for the wedding of the century!

Storyteller: Aladdin and his mother went home to get themselves ready for the wedding. The Genie of the Lamp was kept very busy. He produced fine velvet clothes for Aladdin and dresses of silk for his mother. Aladdin rode to his wedding on a stallion as black as night and his mother travelled in a shining carriage. Afterwards, Aladdin and his bride went off in a jewelled carriage drawn by milk-white horses and servants scattered gold coins in their path. It was the most magnificent wedding procession anyone could remember.

So it is told that a poor washerwoman's son married the daughter of an Emperor. They lived happily together in the marble palace and had many clever and beautiful children. On a shelf inside a locked cupboard in the palace, Aladdin kept the old dented lamp. Nobody was ever allowed to clean or polish it. Aladdin kept the lamp safe so that he would never forget the good luck that brought him his beautiful wife whom he loved with all his heart.

Loki the Mischief Maker

adapted from Norse mythology by Paul Copley

This play is an adaptation, taken from the legends and myths of the Norse gods. You can find many stories about Loki in the Norse myths.

The difficulty with performing this play is that Huggin and Munnin are ravens and Brok is an elf. How do you think you could overcome these problems?

Maybe one idea would be to do perform the script as a radio play. You could find some appropriate music to introduce and end it. You could spend time working out sound effects and scribble them on your scripts so that you get them in the right place, then you could read the play and record it onto a cassette.

There are several stage directions in this play but no one designated Narrator or Storyteller to read them aloud. Work out whether you need to say them, whether you need 'voices off' to say them, or whether you can afford to just read them inside your heads rather than aloud. Don't be afraid to try something out and then change it if it doesn't work.

After the reading, discuss the play and then try and find some more Norse myths that have Loki in them. Is he always the same kind of mischief maker?

Things to talk about:
- Who comes off badly and who comes off well in the script?
- How?
- Why?
- What do you think of Loki and his part in this story?
- Who is your favourite character and why?

Loki the Mischief Maker

adapted by Paul Copley

Cast:

Huggin – a raven
Munnin – another raven
Odin – God of Battle, leader of the gods
Loki – a trickster, son of a giant
Iduna – Lady of Youth, friend of the gods
Thor – God of Thunder, son of Odin
Brok – a Blacksmith Elf

The Norse gods live in the Realm of Asgard. Ordinary mortals live in Midgard. Midgard and Asgard are linked by the Rainbow Bridge, also called Bifrost Bridge. The Frost Giants, who live in far away Jotunheim, are sworn enemies of the Norse gods.

Scene 1	On the Rainbow Bridge

(Enter Huggin and Munnin – two ravens)

Huggin: Phew! My wings are so tired, Munnin!

Munnin: Mine too, Huggin. That was a very long journey.

Huggin: Squawk! We must rest for a moment.

Munnin: Croak! We need to rest. Even my voice is tired.

Huggin: Your voice does sound a bit croaky, Munnin!

Munnin: Of course it does, Huggin. And so does yours. We are both ravens. Ravens croak!

(They laugh croakily and squawkily)

Huggin: It is good to be back home in Asgard, safe and sound!

Munnin: Odin will be pleased with us! We found the Castle of the Storm Giant.

Huggin: And we saw Loki rescue the fair Lady Iduna.

Munnin: Look out! Here comes our master.

(Enter Odin)

Odin: Huggin and Munnin! My trusted friends.

Huggin: Hail to you, Odin! Lord of Asgard!

Munnin: Hail Odin! Master! King of kings!

Odin: Yes, yes, never mind all that. Do you have news for me?

Brilliant Publications – Fun with Plays
Loki the Mischief Maker by Paul Copley

Munnin: Yes, we have news, Odin.

Odin: News of the fair Lady Iduna?

Huggin: Loki has rescued her from the Castle of the Storm Giant.

Munnin: Yes, Loki changed his shape. He changed himself into a big bird, much bigger than us.

Huggin: He changed into a great falcon. He swooped down and snatched Lady Iduna from the castle turret.

Odin: What about the Apples of Youth? Was Lady Iduna holding her basket of Golden Apples?

Huggin: Yes, master, she was.

Munnin:	Loki should return any minute now. But it is a long and tiring journey.
Huggin:	And Loki is carrying a passenger...
Munnin:	... who is carrying golden apples!
Odin:	Look! Here he comes. Oh brave Loki! Can you see him?
Huggin:	Yes I see him. But master, do you see what is following him? Gaining on him?
Munnin:	A giant eagle! What a fearsome creature! Look at his sharp talons!
Odin:	It is the Storm Giant. He has turned himself into a fierce black eagle.
Huggin:	SQUAAAAWK!! Loki is tired. The eagle is going to catch him!
Munnin:	CROOOOAK!! What can we do? What can we do?
Odin:	Wait! Loki has put on speed. He may yet beat the eagle. Quick! We must be ready when he arrives! We must protect the Realm of Asgard! Follow me!

(Odin leaves. Huggin and Munnin squawk to each other and follow Odin)

Scene 2	**Inside Asgard, the Realm of the Gods**

(Odin speaks with Huggin and Munnin)

Odin:	Now, this is the plan. You, my two trusted ravens, must go back to the Gateway of Asgard.
Huggin:	We will.
Munnin:	Come on, Huggin!

Brilliant Publications – Fun with Plays
Loki the Mischief Maker by Paul Copley

Odin: Wait! Listen! As soon as Loki and Lady Iduna are safely inside Asgard you must light the great bonfire in the gateway.

Huggin: Squaaawk! The bonfire will keep out the evil Storm Giant!

Munnin: Croooak! Even a giant eagle as big and black as he cannot fly through a bonfire!

Huggin: Come on, Munnin, quick!

(They leave)

Odin: Loki has managed to trick the Storm Giant. If he arrives safely I must reward him with something suitable, something that befits such bravery.

(Enter Loki and Lady Iduna. Loki is out of breath)

Loki: Hail Odin! Oooh, next time I think of changing myself into a falcon, I must remember that flying is very tiring!

Odin: Brave Loki! Welcome back! And Lady Iduna – welcome!

(They all clasp hands)

Iduna: Oh, that cruel Storm Giant! I thought that I would be imprisoned in his horrible castle for ever. And when he turned himself into that great big black eagle I thought he was going to catch us and tear us to pieces!

Loki: He nearly did. He was flying so fast after us that trees and houses were being uprooted by the wind from his wings.

Iduna: Where is that savage eagle now? Are we safe?

(Enter Huggin and Munnin)

Huggin: SQUAAAAWK!! Good news!

This page may be photocopied for use by the purchasing institution only.

Brilliant Publications – Fun with Plays
Loki the Mischief Maker by Paul Copley

109

Munnin:	CROOOOAK!! The black eagle is dead!
Huggin:	The Storm Giant is no more!
Munnin:	He was flying so fast that he could not stop!
Huggin:	He flew straight into the flames of our bonfire.
Odin:	Well done, my feathered friends!
Huggin:	Squaaawk!
Munnin:	Croooak!
Loki:	No longer will the cruel Storm Giant make war on Asgard and threaten you, great Odin!
Odin:	You are right, Loki! And you have bravely returned the fair Lady Iduna to Asgard.
Iduna:	Thank you, Loki. Brave, wise Loki. Now, great Odin, you can eat my Golden Apples of Youth every day. You and all the other gods of Asgard need never grow old.
Huggin:	Squaaawk! An apple a day...
Munnin:	...keeps old age away! Crooooook!
Odin:	Ha-ha-ha! Come, Lady Iduna.
Iduna:	Thank you, I will. **(She takes Odin's arm)**
Odin:	And Loki, valiant Loki, come with us and claim your reward. From now on you shall not live in Midgard with ordinary mortals.
Loki:	Where am I going to live then, Odin?
Odin:	**(Odin laughs)** Here Loki. You will live here. You shall cross the Rainbow Bridge and live here, with us, in Asgard.

Loki:	Live in Asgard with the gods? Oh, thank you, great one!
Odin:	Tonight we shall hold a feast in your honour. You shall eat of the Apples of Youth. You will live amongst gods and be treated like a god! Come!

(Odin, Iduna and Loki leave)

Huggin:	Odin said 'valiant Loki'! I say 'lucky Loki'! He always wanted to live like a king. He has got exactly what he wanted.
Munnin:	Lady Iduna said 'wise Loki'? I say 'tricky Loki'! I heard that he tricked Lady Iduna into meeting the Storm Giant in the first place!
Huggin:	It is no secret that Loki is a half giant himself!
Munnin:	Asgard had better watch out now that Loki is within its walls.
Huggin:	Loki is a tricksy trickster!
Munnin:	Loki is a crafty customer!
Huggin:	SQUAAAAWK!! Loki is a Mischief Maker!
Munnin:	Odin had better watch out. Because mischief is exactly what Loki will make! CROOOOAK!!

(Huggin and Munnin nod wisely and leave)

Scene 3	**Inside Odin's palace**

(Enter Odin and Loki)

Loki:	Thank you for seeing me, great Odin! I come to you to plead for the release of my son, Fenris.
Odin:	Loki, I cannot allow Fenris to run free.

Loki:	Why not? Fenris is a prisoner on a lonely island. He was put in chains by Thor. Thor is your son. Fenris is my son. How can it be right for your son to imprison my son.
Odin:	Loki, your son Fenris is a wolf! A giant, savage wolf who is a great danger to us all.
Loki:	Fenris is not a danger.
Odin:	Not a danger? Fenris bit off the hand of Tyr, God of War!
Loki:	Only because your son Thor tricked Fenris and tied him to a rock with the magic chain that can never be broken.
Odin:	Tricks? You speak of tricks? You, Loki, the trickiest of tricksters?
Loki:	Me? A trickster?
Odin:	Loki, your tricks are getting us all into trouble. Look at your promise to the builder of the Asgard Wall.
Loki:	I promised to pay him ONLY if he finished building the wall in record time!
Odin:	But you promised to pay, not with money, but by giving him the Sun and the Moon!
Loki:	Well, he never finished the wall. We did not have to pay. I tricked him!
Odin:	You did. But what if he had finished the wall in record time? What then? Loki, what good is a wall to us if we don't have the Sun and the Moon? I am tired of your mischief, Loki!
	(Enter Huggin and Munnin)
Huggin:	SQUAAAAWK! Odin, great Odin! Here comes your son, Thor, God of Thunder!
Munnin:	CROOOOAK! And he is in a thundering bad mood!

Loki:	I think I will go now, Odin.
Odin:	Stay where you are, Loki. Let us see what Thor wants.
Huggin:	We know what he wants!
Munnin:	And we know who he wants!

(Enter Thor, very angry, and Lady Iduna)

Thor:	WHERE IS LOKI? When I find him I will break him into tiny little pieces! WHERE IS HE?
Loki:	Oh dear! **(Loki hides behind Huggin and Munnin)**
Iduna:	There he is. Look. The two crows are hiding him.
Huggin:	SQUAAAWK! We are not hiding him!
Munnin:	CROOOAK! No, we are not hiding him! **(They stand aside)**
Huggin:	And by the way, we are not crows.
Munnin:	No, we are ravens.
Iduna:	Sorry.
Thor:	Never mind all that. Come here to me, Loki. You will make no more mischief when I have finished with you.

(Thor makes a grab at Loki who dodges him)

Odin:	STOP!! Now, what is all this about?
Thor:	He has made mischief for the very last time.
Odin:	What has he done?
Thor:	My lovely wife Sif is bald. She has no hair. That is what he has done!

Huggin:	He has cut off Sif's golden hair.
Munnin:	I did not know Loki was a hairdresser!
Thor:	Stop your squawking and croaking you two!
Odin:	Please will somebody tell me exactly what has happened!
Iduna:	Loki has caused the hair of Thor's lovely wife to fall out!
Thor:	He was angry that Fenris was chained up!
Iduna:	During the night he took revenge on Thor's wife.
Thor:	My wife is bald!
Odin:	No hair left at all?
Thor:	Not one hair left on her head.
Iduna:	Her beautiful shining hair.
Huggin:	Now she has a beautiful shining head.
Munnin:	No hair. Just beautiful shining skin!
Odin:	Be quiet, Huggin and Munnin! What have you to say, Loki?
Loki:	I was angry! I did it because I was angry!
Thor:	Well, now I AM ANGRY! Let me take him away, great Odin. My lightning bolts will take care of him.
Loki:	No, please! Have mercy! I will pay for my mischief. I will do anything for you, Thor. Anything.
Thor:	I will tell you what you will do. You will put back the golden hair on Sif's head. You will put it back and it will grow again! Unless you do that I will grind up your bones and feed you to the ravens.

Huggin:	Ooh no, I do not want his bones!
Munnin:	Me neither!
Loki:	I will do it! I will put back Sif's golden hair!
Thor:	No tricks!
Odin:	How will you do it?
Loki:	I will visit the Blacksmith Elves. The same elves that made the magic chain.
Iduna:	The magic chain that will never break?
Loki:	The chain that binds my son Fenris.
Odin:	The Blacksmith Elves work with all kinds of metal. They can work with gold.
Loki:	I will ask them to spin fine gold thread. They will use their magic powers to make new golden hair for your wife Sif.
Thor:	Will it grow on her head? Will it work?
Loki:	Yes it will.
Thor:	How do you know it will work?
Loki:	Unless you let me go to the Blacksmith Elves, none of us will know what is possible! Let me go, Thor!
Iduna:	Let him try, Thor!
Odin:	Well? Thor?
Thor:	Go to the Blacksmith Elves and come back with my wife's hair. But listen well, Loki. If this is a trick I will find you wherever you are. You will never escape me!
Loki:	Thank you. I will not fail. I go to the Land of the Blacksmith Elves! **(He leaves)**

Iduna:	He has gone.
Thor:	And he had better come back very soon!
Odin:	Huggin, Munnin, follow him. Come back and tell me what happens when he reaches the dark caverns of the Blacksmith Elves!
Huggin:	Squaaaawk!! We will! Come on, Munnin!
Munnin:	Crooooak!!

(They all leave)

Scene 4	Inside the Great Hall of Valhalla

(Enter Huggin and Munnin)

Huggin:	SQUAAAWK!! Bright light and fresh air again! It is good to be home, Munnin!
Munnin:	CROOOAK!! I hate the dark and gloomy caverns of the Blacksmith Elves. Nothing but soot and smoke and showers of sparks!
Huggin:	If only Loki had not met Brok!
Munnin:	If only! We could have been back home days ago!

(Enter Odin)

Odin:	What's that? Has Loki been up to his tricks again?
Huggin:	Hail Odin!
Munnin:	Lord and master...
Odin:	Yes, yes, yes, never mind all that! Tell me what has happened! Did Loki get the magical golden hair for Thor's wife Sif?
Huggin:	Yes, master, he did!

Brilliant Publications – Fun with Plays
Loki the Mischief Maker by Paul Copley

Odin:	Good!
Munnin:	And the Blacksmith Elves gave him two other wonderful presents to bring back to Asgard.
Odin:	So Loki has three wondrous and magical gifts for us? Splendid!
Huggin:	Yes, but then Loki met Brok, a small, sooty blacksmith with yellow spiky teeth!
Munnin:	Brok is a gambler.
Huggin:	Brok is a risk taker.
Munnin:	He told Loki that he, Brok, would make three gifts for the Gods of Asgard. He said they would be far better gifts than Loki's three gifts!
Huggin:	Loki told Brok that it was impossible to make better gifts than his!
Odin:	Oh no! What happened then?
Huggin:	Well, Brok set about making his three gifts.
Munnin:	Loki changed himself into a wasp!
Huggin:	He stung Brok three times to try to stop him working.
Odin:	That is cheating!
Munnin:	But he did not stop Brok. Brok made three enchanted gifts!
Huggin:	Then, he and Loki made a terrible agreement!
Odin:	Wait! Look! Out there in the courtyard. Loki loaded down with presents. And with him a very grimy elf, covered in soot!
Huggin:	SQUAAAWK!! Has the sooty elf got yellow spiky teeth?

This page may be photocopied for use by the purchasing institution only.

Brilliant Publications – Fun with Plays
Loki the Mischief Maker by Paul Copley

117

Odin:	Yes!
Huggin:	That is Brok!
Odin:	Quick! Off you both go. Find Thor and tell everybody to come here to the great Hall of Valhalla! Quickly!
Munnin:	We will, Master! CROOOOAK!!
	(They leave)
Odin:	And here comes the sooty one!
	(Enter Brok)
Brok:	Hello! I am Brok.
Odin:	I am Odin. Welcome to the Realm of Asgard, Brok!
Brok:	Thank you, great Odin.
Odin:	I hear you have brought gifts from the Caverns of the Blacksmiths.
Brok:	Yes. Loki has brought three gifts. I have also brought three gifts.
Odin:	I see. Tell me, Brok, what is the terrible agreement you have made with Loki?
Brok:	Loki and I have agreed this. That if the great Odin thinks Loki's gifts are best, then Loki will win the competition. His prize is my head.
Odin:	You mean, you will let Loki cut off your head?
Brok:	Yes. But if great Odin likes my gifts best, I win.
Odin:	And you cut off Loki's head?
Brok:	That is what we agreed.
Odin:	That is, indeed, a truly terrible agreement! Where is Loki?

Brilliant Publications – Fun with Plays
Loki the Mischief Maker by Paul Copley

(Enter Thor pushing Loki in front of him)

Thor: Here he is, father!

(Loki bows low to Odin)

Loki: Hail to you, great Odin!

Odin: Loki, I know about the competition between you and Brok!

Thor: So do I. I hope Brok wins. I cannot wait to see Loki lose his head.

(Enter Lady Iduna followed by Huggin and Munnin)

Iduna: The first of Loki's gifts is wonderful! Thor's wife Sif has beautiful golden hair once again.

Odin: Good!

Thor: Lucky for you Loki, that your first gift worked so well.

Loki: All my gifts are just as fine as you will now see! Here is my second gift. It is Skidbladnir, the best of all sailing ships!

Huggin: Squaaawk! But it is the size of the toy boat that sails in my bathtub!

Loki: The magic of it is this. It will unfold to carry all the Gods of Asgard swiftly over land or sea!

Munnin: Croooak! That is a truly magical present, Loki!

Loki: Here is my third gift. It is for you, great Odin. It is the enchanted spear called Gungnir. When you throw this spear it will always hit the target!

Odin: Three truly enchanting gifts, Loki.

Loki: Have I won the contest? Shall I cut off Brok's head?

This page may be photocopied for use by the purchasing institution only.

Brilliant Publications – Fun with Plays
Loki the Mischief Maker by Paul Copley

119

Thor: Wait! Not so fast, Loki!

Odin: First, Loki, let us see what Brok has brought to Asgard!

Brok: Three gifts, Lord Odin. I made them all myself. Even when Loki turned himself into a wasp and stung me I never stopped work!

Thor: Cheating as usual, Loki!

Odin: Show your gifts, Brok!

Brok: Here is my first gift. The gift of greatest wealth!

Iduna: Look, everyone. That is a truly beautiful gold ring, Brok!

Brok: Every ninth day, eight more gold rings will fall from it!

Huggin: SQUAAAWK! Never-ending wealth. Better than winning the Asgard lottery, Lord Odin!

Brok: Here is my second gift. The gift of greatest speed!

Iduna:	Look, everyone. A wild pig with shiny steel whiskers. It has a golden mane like a lion!
Brok:	Sit on his back and he will carry you faster than lightning through air or water!
Munnin:	CROOOAK! What a speedy piggy! Faster than any sailing ship, surely!
Brok:	Here is my third gift. The gift of greatest strength!
Thor:	Look at this! A gleaming hammer of great power and beauty!
Brok:	This hammer called Miolnir is for you, Thor. It will always hit its target. It will always return to your hand when you have thrown it. It will destroy your enemies and will never fail you!
Odin:	Loki. Brok. You have each brought to Asgard three wonderful gifts. But of these six gifts, Miolnir the hammer is the one most precious. In the hands of my son Thor, it will keep Asgard safe from the cruel Frost Giants.
Loki:	So. Who has won the competition? Me or Brok!
Odin:	Brok gave us the Hammer of Greatest Strength. Brok wins the contest!
Loki:	I see. Well, good bye everybody! I must dash off now! **(He starts to leave but is stopped by Thor)**
Thor:	No you don't. Stand still! **(Loki stops)** And do not go changing yourself into a wasp. Brok! You can take your prize!
Loki:	What? You will let Brok cut off my head?
Brok:	That is what we agreed. **(Brok raises his sword)**
Huggin:	Squawk! I can't look!

This page may be photocopied for use by the purchasing institution only.

Brilliant Publications – Fun with Plays
Loki the Mischief Maker by Paul Copley

121

Munnin:	Croak! I can't either!
Loki:	Wait! Brok, remember what we agreed! If you win you may cut off my head.
Brok:	Yes. And I've won. Hold still!
Loki:	But remember this also! My NECK is mine. You can't have any of my neck!
Brok:	What?
Loki:	My head is yours. Not my neck!
Brok:	I cannot cut off your head without taking some of your neck as well!
Loki:	Then you cannot cut off my head! Sorry, Brok! Shake hands!
Brok:	You have tricked me with words. Loki has tricked me with words, Lord Odin!
Odin:	Loki tricks everybody he meets, Brok!
Brok:	Then I know what to do with him. **(Brok walks up to Loki and puts his finger to Loki's lips)**
Loki:	What are you doing, Brok?
Brok:	Sewing up your lips with magic thread!
Loki:	What? Stop him somebody!
Brok:	There! Now you will never be able to trick anybody with words again!
Loki:	Mmmmmmm! MMMMMMM!! MMMMMMM!!
Brok:	Good bye everybody. I must get back to my smithy!
Odin:	Good bye Brok!

Brilliant Publications – Fun with Plays
Loki the Mischief Maker by Paul Copley

(They all shout 'good bye' as Brok leaves)

Loki: MMMMMM!! MMMMMM!!

Thor: He cannot speak! Trickster, mischief maker, it serves you right!

Huggin: Squaaawk!! Tell us a joke then, Loki!

Loki: MMMMMMMM!!

Munnin: Croooak!! Sing us a song then, Loki!

Loki: MMMMMMMM!!

(They all chuckle)

Odin: Loki the trickster has got what he deserves for once! Now he will fnd it difficult to make his mischief! Come, let us eat and drink and be very, very merry. Come, everybody!

(They all leave following Odin. All, that is, except Loki)

Loki: They've all gone! And they all think that Brok's magic thread sewed up my lips. Good! Let them think Brok's magic worked. If they believe that I cannot speak, I can say whatever I like. I can whisper all kinds of mischief into their ears and no one will know it is me! Teee-heee! I can make lots more mischief now! Teee-heee-heee! **(He starts to leave calling)** HEY! WAIT FOR ME! WAIT FOR ME!! **(quietly)** Ooops! I mean **(calling)** Mmmm-mmm-mm!! Mmmm-mmm-mm!! **(He leaves)**

Dog in the Car

by Irene Yates

This is the kind of story that could happen to any family, any Saturday morning.

To perform it, all you would need is four chairs facing forward for the car and two facing backwards for the boot. You'd have to set these sideways on to the audience so that the car looked as though it were parked at the kerb. You could make some sort of frame to be Nazeem's front door, and the only other things you'd really need are a few hand props. You could have people dressed in black to move the 'car' when it drives off. You would have the family first sitting on the seats, Dad turning on the ignition, then the family would stand up, the chair movers would pick up the chairs, and everyone would move off together, at the same pace, to show the car moving. Decide for yourself whether you would want somebody to act being the dog, or whether you could:

a)   use some kind of bean-bag dog or furry toy, or,

b)   all act as though the dog is there even though there is nothing. This is probably the harder option because it means the actors have all got to focus on the same spot and somehow make the audience believe that they can see the dog. It would be fun to have 'neighbours' coming out and gathering round to watch.

Things to talk about:
- What can you tell about the different characters from the dialogue?
- What would you do if this kind of thing happened to you?

Dog in the Car

by Irene Yates

Cast:
Narrator
Dad
Tom
Mum
Nazeem's mum
Karli
Nazeem's dad

Narrator:	It's a Saturday and the Prince family are going to town to do the shopping. Tom doesn't want to go.
Dad:	Come on, jump to it!
Tom:	Why do I have to go? I hate shopping.
Dad:	Tough. You can't stay here by yourself and we're all going.
Mum:	Oh come on, Tom, we haven't got time to mess about. We've got to pick Karli up from Nazeem's house.
Tom:	Why can't I stop and play with MY friends?
Mum:	**(patiently)** Because you've got to go to the dentist afterwards.
Tom:	But shopping's so boring.
Mum:	Shopping's not boring.
Tom:	Yes it is. Boring. Boring. Boring.
Dad:	Life's boring, Tom. You get used to it after a bit.
Tom:	Well – I don't want it to be boring. I want it to be good and exciting.
Mum:	**(running out of patience…)** Just get in the car!
Dad:	**(run out of patience!)** NOW!
Narrator:	Tom gives up. He knows when he's beaten. Reluctantly he climbs in and off they go. They get to Nazeem's house and stop the car.
Dad:	**(to Tom)** Go and knock on the door and fetch Karli.
Tom:	Why me?
Mum:	Oh for goodness' sake! Just go.

Brilliant Publications – Fun with Plays
Dog in the Car by Irene Yates

Tom:	But I don't see why...
Dad:	Do you have to argue with EVERYTHING?
Tom:	I'm not arguing, I'm just saying...
Mum:	Oh – I'll go myself. **(To Dad)** Open the boot, to put her bag in.
Tom:	**(muttering)** I didn't say I WOULDN'T go...
Dad:	If you just did as you were told straight away instead of having to argue…
Tom:	It's not ME arguing. It's Mum.
Narrator:	Dad sighs, gets out of the car and goes round to open the boot. He lifts the boot. Mum's on the step talking to Nazeem's mum.
Mum:	**(calling to him)** Come and get Karli's bag for her.
Narrator:	Dad goes along the path.
Dad:	**(to Nazeem's mum)** Hi. Hope she's been good.
Nazeem's mum:	She's been fine, they were giggling all night!
Narrator:	Just then there's a shout from the car.
Tom:	Dad! Dad! Quick.
Narrator:	They all turn round quickly and rush down the path to see what's happening. Tom's hanging out of the car window.
Tom:	It wasn't my fault! It's nothing to do with me!
Mum:	What isn't?
Tom:	The dog. It's not my fault.

This page may be photocopied for use
by the purchasing institution only.

Brilliant Publications – Fun with Plays
Dog in the Car by Irene Yates

127

Mum/Dad/ Nazeem's mum:	What dog?
Tom:	The dog in the boot! It just jumped in!
Narrator:	They all rush round to the back of the car. There, sitting in the boot, slobbering at them, is a massive German Shepherd Dog.
Mum:	Oh no!
Dad:	Don't worry. I'll soon get it out. **(to Nazeem's mum)** Do you know who it belongs to?
Nazeem's mum:	I've never seen it before in my life! It doesn't live round here.
Mum:	Are you sure?
Dad:	It's got a collar on.
Nazeem's mum:	No, it definitely doesn't belong to anybody in this street.
Tom:	I suppose you'll blame me, but I didn't do anything, honest. I didn't even speak to it.
Dad:	**(to the dog)** Come on. Nice doggy.
Narrator:	The dog looks at him and gives a loud bark.
Mum:	It doesn't like you.
Dad:	Don't be daft. It was barking to say hello.
Mum:	Oh yes?
Dad:	You watch. I'll soon get it out.
Narrator:	He puts his hand towards the dog. The dog lowers its head and growls. Dad snatches his hand away.
Tom:	Don't worry. I'll get it out.

Brilliant Publications – Fun with Plays
Dog in the Car by Irene Yates

Narrator:	Tom gets out of the car and comes round to the boot. The dog lies down, head on its paws.
Tom:	Hello. You're a nice dog – aren't you?
Narrator:	The dog growls. Just then Karli and Nazeem come out. Nazeem sees the dog and scoots back in the house, frightened.
Nazeem's mum:	She doesn't like dogs.
Mum:	Neither do I that much.
Karli:	He's a lovely dog.
Dad:	You get him out then.
Karli:	Come on, boy.
Narrator:	The dog growls.
Nazeem's dad:	I don't think it's going to be so easy, somehow.
Karli:	I think he needs time to get to know us.
Tom:	He probably feels crowded with everybody round him. Perhaps he's frightened.
Mum:	He doesn't look very frightened to me.
Nazeem's mum:	Nor me.
Nazeem's dad:	Tom's got a point though, hasn't he? Perhaps if everybody wasn't here, he'd come out.
Mum:	What do you think we should do then?
Nazeem's dad:	Tell you what – you all get in the car, and be ready to go. I'll coax the dog out and when he's out I'll close your boot and off you go.
Nazeem's mum:	**(anxiously)** That leaves us standing here with a strange, fierce dog.

This page may be photocopied for use by the purchasing institution only.

Brilliant Publications – Fun with Plays
Dog in the Car by Irene Yates

129

Nazeem's dad:	He's not a fierce dog. What makes you think he's fierce?
Nazeem's mum:	He looks fierce to me.
Nazeem's dad:	I don't think so, you're just a scaredy...
Narrator:	The dog growls hard and fast. Then he sits up and starts barking.
Tom:	He knows you're talking about him.
Karli:	Well, why wouldn't we be talking about him? He's stuck in our car...
Tom:	Yes, but we shouldn't be talking about him, should we? We'll only upset him!
Dad:	Tom – get in the car. Karli! Mum! Go on, me and Nazeem's dad will sort this out.
Narrator:	They all look at each other.
Tom:	But I don't want...
Dad:	Tom!
Narrator:	Mum, Karli and Tom get in the car. The dog lies down again.
Nazeem's dad:	See? He definitely feels happier when there aren't so many people around him.
Nazeem's mum:	I'll get in the car as well.
Nazeem's dad:	That's no good is it? If you get in the car and I get him out they can't drive off with you as well, can they?
Dad:	I'll get in the car then.
Nazeem's dad:	Good. Okay.
Narrator:	Dad gets in the car. Nazeem's dad starts to try and encourage the dog to get out.

Nazeem's dad:	Come on then, good old boy.
Narrator:	The dog eyes him but doesn't move.
Nazeem's mum:	What about if I fetched him some meat or something?
Nazeem's dad:	That's a good idea. What have you got?
Nazeen's mum:	I've got steak that you were having for your tea.
Nazeem's dad:	Oh well, it'll be worth it if we get him out. Go and fetch it.
Narrator:	Nazeem's mum goes off. Dad shouts from inside the car.
Dad:	Any luck yet?
Nazeem's dad:	No. But we've had a good idea. We're getting him some meat to TEMPT him out.
Narrator:	Nazeem's mum comes back with the meat.
Nazeem's mum:	Here we are.

Narrator:	She holds the meet out gingerly. The dog pushes his nose forward and sniffs at it. Nazeem's mum thinks he's going to bite her. She gives a little yelp and throws the meat into the car at the dog. The dog eats the meat.
Nazeem's dad:	Now look what you've done. That was clever, wasn't it?
Nazeem's mum:	Well you should have done it if you could do it any better.
Narrator:	They both stand there, watching the dog licking its chops.
Nazeem's dad:	Well, there's one thing. He enjoyed the meat.
Nazeem's mum:	There's nothing for your tea now.
Narrator:	Nazeem's dad looks a bit unhappy at this news. Dad gets out of the car and comes round to the back.
Dad:	Your idea didn't work then?
Nazeem's dad:	(dolefully) Unfortunately not.
Narrator:	Mum and Karli get out of the car and come round to the back.
Dad:	What do we do now then?
Nazeem's mum:	You might as well come in and have a cup of tea. Perhaps if we all leave him he might get out.
Mum:	Well we can't just leave the car open, can we?
Karli:	Why not? The dog's guarding it.
Dad:	Yes. But if he GOES, which is what we want him to do – the car'll be sitting here on its own, wide open.
Karli:	Tom could guard it.

 Brilliant Publications – Fun with Plays
Dog in the Car by Irene Yates

Narrator:	Tom hears this and gets out of the car.
Tom:	You're not leaving me in the car on my own with this... this... wild beast!
Dad:	**(by now he's had enough!)** Well, we'll all stay here then.
Nazeem's mum:	I'll go and make the tea and bring it outside.
Narrator:	The dog glares at them all, growling.
Nazeem's dad:	I've got an idea. Perhaps it just wants to go for a ride.
Dad:	Now that IS an idea. Perhaps it's used to getting in the boot of its owner's car and it thinks we'll take it for a ride.
Tom:	Good thinking, Batman. Perhaps if we took it for a ride and brought it back it'd just get out.
Narrator:	The two dads and Tom look at each other, each thinking this is a good idea. Dad shuts the boot of the car, and they all get in. Off they go.
Mum:	I don't know. What a performance!
Karli:	It'll be all right, Mum. By the time they get back the dog will have had enough, and he'll just get out.
Narrator:	Nazeem's mum comes back with the tea. Several neighbours come out to see what's going on. The two mums and Karli stand on the pavement looking out for the car to come back. At last it comes round the corner. The car draws up beside them. The two dads and Tom all jump out together. Dad runs round to the boot, opens it.
Dad:	There you are then, boy. Home again!
Narrator:	The dog just looks at them. Then it barks. Then it puts its head down and growls.

Dad:	Now what?
Tom:	I think we should phone the police.
Mum:	What for?
Tom:	Ask them what to do.
Dad:	Perhaps we should phone the car rescue.
Nazeem's mum:	I don't think they rescue dogs from cars. I think they only come if you've broken down.
Narrator:	Everybody looks down at the pavement. The dog barks.
Dad:	Perhaps Tom's right.
Narrator:	Tom beams.
Nazeem's dad:	I'll go and phone them.
Dad:	What are you going to say?
Nazeem's dad:	I'll just tell them a strange, fierce dog jumped into your boot and we can't get him out.
Dad:	Simple as that.
Narrator:	Nazeem's dad goes off to make the phone call. The rest of them drink their tea and try, in turns, to coax the dog out of the car. It just glares at them.
Mum:	If we could get its collar and see where it lived...
Nazeem's mum:	I wouldn't if I were you. It nearly had my hand off when I gave it the meat.
Dad:	I expect it was hungry.
Tom:	You shouldn't have fed it really. Because now it probably thinks you'll feed it again and it won't go away.

Dad:	All right, Tom. Don't be rude.
Tom:	Yes but...
Nazeem's mum:	He's probably right.
Narrator:	Nazeem's dad comes back.
Nazeem's dad:	Right, that's that then.
Dad:	What did they say?
Nazeem's dad:	They want you to drive over to the police station. They said whatever you do, don't touch the dog in case it goes for you. They're sending for the dog handler. When you get to the police station, the dog handler will get it out.
Mum:	I don't fancy getting in the car with that thing in.
Tom:	It won't hurt you.
Karli:	Oh no?
Tom:	No, it's just...
Dad:	Tom! Get in the car!
Narrator:	They all get in the car. They drive off with Nazeem's mum and dad watching them. The dog looks at them out of the back window as they drive off. It pants in the back of the car all the way to the police station. When they get there Dad pulls the car into the car park.
Dad:	Now look – somebody go in and tell them...
Tom:	I'll go.
Dad:	No you won't, you're not old enough. They'll think you're messing about.
Tom:	No they won't.

This page may be photocopied for use by the purchasing institution only.

Brilliant Publications – Fun with Plays
Dog in the Car by Irene Yates

135

Dad:	They will.
Tom:	They won't
Mum:	Oh for goodness' sake, Tom! I'll come with you. We'll go together.
Karli:	Well, I'm staying here.
Dad:	I'll get out and open the boot. Listen to the dog panting. It's sweating like a trooper.
Karli:	It stinks!
Dad:	It needs a bit of fresh air, that's all.
Karli:	Well, I'm not staying in the car with it. I'll get out with you.
Mum:	Okay – we all get out. Tom and me go in, you two stop here.
Narrator:	They all get out of the car. Mum and Tom go towards the police station. Dad and Karli go round to the boot. Dad opens the boot. The dog gives a yelp, leaps out of the car and takes off.
Dad:	Oh no!
Narrator:	Mum and Tom turn round to see what's happening.

Karli:	It's gone!
Dad:	Get it back, quick! Here, boy!
Narrator:	But the dog has disappeared.
Dad:	Now what?
Mum:	Let's go. Quick.
Dad:	We can't do that. They were sending for the dog handler.
Karli:	They'll wonder where we are.
Tom:	Well, they won't know, will they. We could just go.
Mum:	No, we can't. It's not right.
Dad:	No. We'll have to go in and tell them what's happened. Come on. All of us together.
Tom:	But...
Dad:	No buts. Come on.
Tom:	Can't I just stay here?
Dad:	No you can't. We're all going in.
Mum:	Stop making a fuss and just get going.
Tom:	It's not me making a fuss.
Mum:	Yes, it is.
Dad:	Tom – IN!
Narrator:	Reluctantly, Tom follows them across the car park.
Mum:	**(muttering to Dad)** We're not going to have time to do any shopping at this rate.
Tom:	**(punches the air in triumph)** No shopping! Yeah! Thanks, Dog. You see, Dad? Life's full of surprises...

The Ghost of Sir Hubert

by Stan Barrett

This script will give you an introduction to A MIDSUMMER NIGHT'S DREAM by William Shakespeare. You will notice that some of the speeches, or parts of some of the speeches, are in bold type. This is because they are quotations from A MIDSUMER NIGHT'S DREAM.

One of the things that would help you to read this script is to go through it and highlight all the quotations so that you can find them easily. Then when you come across them they won't take you by surprise.

In a way there are two plays here – the first play is what is happening with the children, the second play is the bits from Shakespeare. You will need to be able to decide which is which and the highlighting will help you.

Things to talk about:

■ Do you think 'spooky bits' work well in an ordinary setting? What is it that makes them work? How can you make them even spookier for your audience when you are reading the play aloud?

■ What do you think you have learned about the play A MIDSUMMER NIGHT'S DREAM, by William Shakespeare, from what happens in The GHOST OF SIR HUBERT?

■ How can you tell, when you are reading the play, which bits of text are quotations from Shakespeare?

The Ghost of Sir Hubert

by Stan Barrett

Cast: **Narrator**
Damien
Dave
Jo
Mrs Reed
Statue

Narrator:	There is a room at the back of the library. It is full of old books. Standing in the shadows is a statue of a boy.
Mrs Reed:	Follow me.
	(Enter Damien, Jo and Dave. They don't see the statue)
Damien:	It's a bit dark in here.
Jo:	And dusty.
Dave:	It's creepy.
Mrs Reed:	It's just an old store room. We might find that book in here. It should be in one of these cardboard boxes.
	(Mrs Reed walks by the boxes looking at their numbers)
Mrs Reed:	This is the one.
Narrator:	They help Mrs Reed to lift the box down to the floor. They start taking the books out.
Mrs Reed:	**(as they search)** Why do you want A MIDSUMMER NIGHT'S DREAM?
Jo:	We want it for a competition at school.
Dave:	We've got a speech from a play.
Jo:	But all the full stops and commas are missing.
Damien:	We've got to put them back.
Jo:	I found out it's from A MIDSUMMER NIGHT'S DREAM.
Dave:	I found out it's by William Shakespeare.
Damien:	And I thought of coming here.

Dave:	So we're going to share the prize if we win.
Mrs Reed:	I think someone got here before you. They've taken our last copy.
Narrator:	By now, the box is nearly empty.
Mrs Reed:	If it's not in this box, then we haven't got it.
Jo:	There's just one book left. **(Pause)** This is it! A MIDSUMMER NIGHT'S DREAM!
Damien and Dave:	YES!
Mrs Reed:	That's good. Now we'll put the other books back.
Narrator:	Damien is soon bored. He wanders into the corner.
Damien:	Look at this statue! Who's it supposed to be?
Dave:	**(joining Damien)** There's some writing next to its feet. It's too dirty. I can't make it out...
Jo:	Move over. Let me look. It says... **(She rubs with her finger)** Sir... Hubert... Chapman... as a boy...
Damien:	Who's he?
Mrs Reed:	**(still putting books back in the box)** Don't you know? Sir Hubert Chapman was the greatest man ever born in this town.
Jo:	Look. It says: 'Sir Hubert Chapman as a boy playing the part of Puck... in... in... ' **(Pause)** Hey! You won't believe this... 'IN A MIDSUMMER NIGHT'S DREAM'! He must have been an actor.
Mrs Reed:	He was. He was brilliant. Even better when he grew up.
Narrator:	Suddenly, a wind whistles through the room.

This page may be photocopied for use by the purchasing institution only.

Brilliant Publications – Fun with Plays
The Ghost of Sir Hubert by Stan Barrett

141

Statue:	**I'll put a girdle round the earth In forty minutes.**
Mrs Reed:	Who said that?
Narrator:	The dim lights flicker on and off.
Damien:	Hey! What's happening?
Narrator:	The lights go out.
Dave:	I can't see!
Jo:	Me neither.
Mrs Reed:	It's all right. Follow my voice.
Jo:	OUCH! That was my foot you trod on!
Damien:	Sorry.
Mrs Reed:	This way.
Dave:	Wow! It's gone cold.
Jo:	I'm shivering!
Damien:	I'm freezing!
Narrator:	The wind drops.
Dave:	Listen. What's that?
Narrator:	They hear quick, light footsteps.
Mrs Reed:	Keep still!
Jo:	We ARE still.
Mrs Reed:	Then who's that?
Narrator:	The footsteps stop.

Dave: If it wasn't us, then who was it?

Mrs Reed: Hello! Is anybody there?

Narrator: No answer. Slowly, they find they can see again.

Jo: The statue! Look! IT'S MOVED!

Narrator: The statue has stepped off its stone block.

(The statue now stands in the centre of the stage)

Dave: The light. It's coming from the statue! Can you see it? It's glowing!

Damien: It's getting brighter.

Jo: And brighter.

Narrator: The statue stands as still as a rock.

Mrs Reed: Did any of you say: 'I'll put a girdle round the earth'?

Dave: Not me.

Jo: Nor me.

Damien: Me neither.

Mrs Reed: But we all heard it. Wait a minute! What date is it?

Dave: It's the 24th of June.

Jo: That's Midsummer's Day, isn't it?

Mrs Reed: That's right! Midsummer's Day! Perhaps my father was right! And I never believed it!

Narrator: Mrs Reed is so excited that she keeps pacing about.

Damien: Never believed what?

This page may be photocopied for use by the purchasing institution only.

Brilliant Publications – Fun with Plays
The Ghost of Sir Hubert by Stan Barrett **143**

Mrs Reed:	Well, my father thought the ghost of Sir Hubert was trapped inside the statue.
Narrator:	The three look at the statue, then move away from it.
Mrs Reed:	And every Midsummer's Day, the statue speaks lines from A MIDSUMMER NIGHT'S DREAM.
Jo:	**(nervously)** Why?
Mrs Reed:	My father said he has to make the last speech of the play. Only then can Sir Hubert's ghost escape from the statue. Then he can go home – wherever that is!
Dave:	**(he is scared)** I think we should go home.
Damien:	**(he is more scared)** Me too. Come on, Dave.
Mrs Reed:	But now we've got the book we could save Sir Hubert?
Jo:	Come back you two! You're chicken!
Dave:	**(to Damien)** Do you want to save Sir Hubert?
Damien:	All right, but why do we need the book?
Mrs Reed:	When the statue pauses, it needs a cue so that it can carry on.
Damien:	O.K. Line up behind me.
Jo:	A cue, not a queue!
Damien:	Eh?
Jo:	A cue is the last few words before the next actor speaks.
Damien:	Pardon?
Mrs Reed:	Let's show him.

Narrator: She points to a page in the book. She tells Damien to read a sentence out loud.

Damien: Which one? This one? **Are you not he?**

(When the statue speaks, he leaps about from person to person. When he stops speaking, he goes back into a freeze. This means he keeps absolutely still)

Statue: **Thou speakest aright:**
I am that merry wanderer of the night.
I jest to Oberon, and make him smile...

Mrs Reed: **(interrupting)** It worked! It worked! **(Sees the statue going back into a freeze)** Oh dear. If we interrupt, he stops speaking.

Dave: Who's Oberon?

Damien: Who's Puck?

This page may be photocopied for use by the purchasing institution only.

Brilliant Publications – Fun with Plays
The Ghost of Sir Hubert by Stan Barrett

145

Mrs Reed:	Puck is a naughty little spirit who lives in woods. His other name is Robin Goodfellow. He is Oberon's messenger.
Dave:	Yes, but who is Oberon?
Jo:	I know! Oberon is the king of the spirits.
Mrs Reed:	That's right. And he's had a row with Titania.
Jo:	She's the fairy queen.
Mrs Reed:	So Oberon tells Puck to put some magic love-juice on Titania's eyelid. When she wakes she will fall in love with whatever she sees first.
Jo:	Can I read a cue?
Mrs Reed:	All right. Try this one. **(She points to a page in the book)**
Jo:	Er... This is Oberon. He is wondering what happened to Titania. Er... Enter Puck. Oberon says: **Here comes my messenger. How now, mad spirit!** **(Before Jo can say any more, the statue leaps into life)**
Statue:	**My Mistress with a monster is in love.**
Damien:	A monster?
Mrs Reed and Jo:	DAMIEN!
Dave:	You interrupted him!
Damien:	Look. It's all right. He's carrying on.
Statue:	**When in that moment, so it came to pass, Titania wak'd, and straightway lov'd an ass.** **(The statue goes back into a freeze)**
Mrs Reed:	I think he jumped to the end of the speech.

Jo: So what DID Titania fall in love with?

Mrs Reed: A man called Bottom. He is wearing an ass's head.

Damien: BOTTOM?

Narrator: Mrs Reed tells them that Bottom is a working man. He and his friends are in the woods to practise a play. They hope to show their play at a royal wedding.

Mrs Reed: They have written it themselves and it's terrible. It's meant to be serious. They try so hard, but do it badly and it's very funny.

Jo: Why has Bottom got an ass's head?

Mrs Reed: Puck put it on him, then scared his friends away. That was to make sure Titania would see Bottom first when she woke up.

Damien: Hang on. If we're trying to save Sir Hubert, why don't we go straight to the end of the play?

Dave: That's right. Then he can say the last speech and go home. Can I say the cue?

Narrator: Mrs Reed finds the end of the play and points to the page.

Dave: Just a minute. Let me look at it first... **(Pause)** It says:
Trip away; make no stay;
Meet me all by break of day.

Statue: **If we shadows have offended,**
Think but this, and all is mended,
That you have but slumbered here.
While these visions did appear.

Damien: Hey! This is our speech, isn't it?

(The statue freezes)

This page may be photocopied for use by the purchasing institution only.

Brilliant Publications – Fun with Plays
The Ghost of Sir Hubert by Stan Barrett

147

Dave and Jo:	DAMIEN!
Dave:	You've done it again!
Jo:	And I was listening to the pauses. We could have won the competition!
Mrs Reed:	And what about Sir Hubert? He's still trapped.
Damien:	Look! It's all right.
Dave:	He's moving again!
Statue:	**Give me your hands, if we be friends,** **And Robin shall restore amends.**
Mrs Reed:	He's done it! That's the end of the speech! He said: 'Give me your hands.' Let's give him a clap! **(As they clap the statue gives each of them a deep bow)**
Narrator:	Then his glow starts to fade. Soon, it is as black as night.
Jo:	Help! I can't see a thing!
Mrs Reed:	Everybody keep still.
Dave:	I can feel something on my face!
Narrator:	It is a soft, warm breeze that passes through the room.
Damien:	Listen.
Narrator:	They hear the footsteps again. Then they hear the voice of the statue. It comes from a distance.
Statue:	Thank you. All of you.
Narrator:	The lights flicker and come on again. The statue is back on its stone block. It looks as if it never moved.

Damien:	Wow! We did it!
Jo:	Why didn't you read any cues, Mrs Reed?
Mrs Reed:	Because my father said that only children could do it.
Damien:	Thanks, Mrs Reed.
Jo:	That was great.
Dave:	Can we go now?
Mrs Reed:	**(she is staring at the statue)** Yes. Of course you can...
Narrator:	When the children have gone, Mrs Reed realises they have forgotten to take the book. She looks at the statue again, then steps back in surprise.

Mrs Reed:	**(to audience)** I'm sure that statue just winked at me. Perhaps he's glad to be rid of the ghost of Sir Hubert... **(She shakes her head)** I think it's time I went home...
	(Exit Mrs Reed)
Narrator:	A few minutes later, Mrs Reed wakes up. She is at home in her own bed. It was all a dream. A MIDSUMMER NIGHT'S DREAM.

What happens when?

- ■ Read the play through very carefully, two or three times.
- ■ Work out the chronological run of the play – the order in which things happen.
- ■ Make notes of all the things that happen, in their right order.

_____

_____

_____

_____

_____

_____

_____

_____

_____

_____

_____

_____

_____

_____

_____

EXTRA!

Choose a scene that you really like. Write it in your own words. You may do this in rhyme or in ordinary narrative text.

Who's who?

■ Read the playscript very carefully. Do a small simple sketch of each character, working out as much as you can from the text about each personality.

EXTRA!

Write a few sentences saying which character you most identify with – that means, the character you would most like to be. Say why.

Role play

- Read the playscript very carefully.
- Take on the role of one of the characters. It can be the one you read aloud, or a different one.
- Retell the story of this play, as though it WERE a story rather than a script.
- Tell it through the eyes of the character you have taken on. Introduce yourself as the character to begin with.

_____

_____

_____

_____

_____

_____

_____

_____

_____

_____

_____

_____

_____

_____

EXTRA!
Still in the role of your chosen character, write a paragraph about one
of the other characters.

Brilliant Publications – Fun with Plays
Worksheet

Extra! Extra! Read all about it!

■ Imagine that the play is reality. You are a reporter for the DAILY BLURB and the plot is a very big, hot news item. Write up your report, as though you have just interviewed one or more of the characters.

■ Give your report a good strong headline and organize your story into paragraphs. Make it as hard-hitting as you can.

_____

_____

_____

_____

_____

_____

_____

_____

_____

_____

_____

_____

_____

EXTRA!
Write six different headlines, then underline the one you like best.

Bits I like...

- Choose six bits of dialogue that you really like.
- Write them out and explain, beside each, what you like about them.

_____

_____

_____

_____

_____

_____

_____

_____

_____

_____

_____

_____

_____

_____

EXTRA!

Choose one of the characters. Write a few sentences which explain how the author manages to convey what this character is like in his or her speeches.

_____

Plan the play!

■ Discuss the play with the others in your group. Think about the characters, the setting and the plot.

■ Imagine you are the author and you are going to write the play. Make a plan to show how you will write it.

_____

_____

_____

_____

_____

_____

_____

_____

_____

_____

_____

_____

_____

_____

_____

_____

EXTRA!
Draw a small simple sketch of one of the characters.

Storytime

- Read the play carefully. Make notes as you read it, showing all the events that happen, in their correct order.
- When you are sure that you have all the notes written as a plan, or synopsis, rewrite the script as a story.

_____

_____

_____

_____

_____

_____

_____

_____

_____

_____

_____

_____

_____

_____

_____

_____

_____

EXTRA!
Write a paragraph telling what might happen next.

What happens next?

■   Think about what might happen next.

■   Write a scene, in the same style as the play, showing what happens. You
     may have to introduce new characters.

_____

_____

_____

_____

_____

_____

_____

_____

_____

_____

_____

_____

_____

_____

EXTRA!
Write a short description of each of your new characters.

Be a director!

- Look carefully at the different scenes in the playscript.
- Give a description of how you would set up each scene if you were directing it on stage.

  Make a list of all the props you would need.

Scene number	How I would set it up	Props needed

- Choose to be one of the characters.
- As that character, write a letter to a friend, telling exactly what happened in the 'play'.
- Remember to tell what happened from your chosen character's point of view.

Dear

_____

_____

_____

_____

_____

_____

_____

_____

_____

_____

from

EXTRA!
Write a letter from your friend, in reply to yours.

This page may be photocopied for use
by the purchasing institution only.

Brilliant Publications – Fun with Plays
Worksheet **159**

Published by   Brilliant Publications,
                      1 Church View,
                      Sparrow Hall Farm,
                      Edlesborough,
                      Dunstable,
                      Bedfordshire.
                      LU6 2ES

                      Telephone: 01525 229720
                      Fax: 01525 229725
                      website: www.brilliantpublications.co.uk
                      e-mail: sales@brilliantpublications.co.uk

Edited by Irene Yates
Illustrated by Frank Endersby

ISBN 1–897675–65–8
First published in 2000
Reprinted in England by Lightning Source 2004
10 9 8 7 6 5 4 3

Lightning Source UK Ltd.
Milton Keynes UK
15 October 2009

144983UK00001B/20/A